Feng Shui

FOR

SUCCESS

Feng Shui

FOR

SUCCESS

Simple Principles for
a Healthy Home and
Prosperous Business

KURT TESKE

Illustrations by Bil Leaf

Jeremy P. Tarcher/Penguin · a member of Penguin Group (USA) Inc. · New York

JEREMY P. TARCHER/PENGUIN
Published by the Penguin Group
Penguin Group (USA) Inc., 375 Hudson Street, New York, New York 10014, USA •
Penguin Group (Canada), 90 Eglinton Avenue East, Suite 700, Toronto, Ontario M4P 2Y3,
Canada (a division of Pearson Canada Inc.) • Penguin Books Ltd, 80 Strand, London
WC2R 0RL, England • Penguin Ireland, 25 St Stephen's Green, Dublin 2, Ireland (a division
of Penguin Books Ltd) • Penguin Group (Australia), 250 Camberwell Road, Camberwell,
Victoria 3124, Australia (a division of Pearson Australia Group Pty Ltd) • Penguin Books
India Pvt Ltd, 11 Community Centre, Panchsheel Park, New Delhi–110 017, India •
Penguin Group (NZ), 67 Apollo Drive, Rosedale, North Shore 0632, New Zealand
(a division of Pearson New Zealand Ltd) • Penguin Books (South Africa) (Pty) Ltd,
24 Sturdee Avenue, Rosebank, Johannesburg 2196, South Africa

Penguin Books Ltd, Registered Offices: 80 Strand, London WC2R 0RL, England

Copyright © 2009 by Kurt Teske
Illustrations by Bil Leaf
All rights reserved. No part of this book may be reproduced, scanned, or distributed in any
printed or electronic form without permission. Please do not participate in or encourage piracy
of copyrighted materials in violation of the author's rights. Purchase only authorized editions.
Published simultaneously in Canada

Excerpt from "East Coker" in *Four Quartets*, copyright 1940 by T. S. Eliot and renewed
1968 by Esme Valerie Eliot, reprinted by permission of Houghton Mifflin Harcourt
Publishing Company.

Most Tarcher/Penguin books are available at special quantity discounts for bulk purchase
for sales promotions, premiums, fund-raising, and educational needs. Special books or book
excerpts also can be created to fit specific needs. For details, write Penguin Group (USA) Inc.
Special Markets, 375 Hudson Street, New York, NY 10014.

Library of Congress Cataloging-in-Publication Data

Teske, Kurt.
Feng shui for success : seven principles for a healthy home and prosperous
business / Kurt Teske.
p.   cm.
Includes bibliographical references and index.
ISBN 978-1-58542-750-5
1. Feng shui.   I. Title.
BF1779.F4T42   2009   2009028960
133.3'337—dc22

Printed in the United States of America
1   3   5   7   9   10   8   6   4   2

Book design by Claire Vaccaro

Neither the publisher nor the author is engaged in rendering professional advice or services
to the individual reader. The ideas, procedures, and suggestions contained in this book are
not intended as a substitute for consulting with a physician. All matters regarding your health
require medical supervision. Neither the author nor the publisher shall be liable or responsible
for any loss or damage allegedly arising from any information or suggestions in this book.

While the author has made every effort to provide accurate telephone numbers and Internet
addresses at the time of publication, neither the publisher nor the author assumes any
responsibility for errors, or for changes that occur after publication. Further, the publisher
does not have any control over and does not assume any responsibility for author or third-party
websites or their content.

CONTENTS

FEB 09 2010

Feng
Shui

FOR

SUCCESS

INTRODUCTION

ention the Chinese words *feng shui* among friends these days, and there's a good chance at least a few have heard of it. Some might even claim to know what it is, something like moving the sofa or placing a funny-shaped mirror on the wall so the universe will then put a Mercedes-Benz on their doorstep. However, it's much more—it's a proven and practical way to enhance life by creating harmony, balance, and vitality in our surroundings. It is a practical application of **Taoism**, one of the oldest and most long-lasting spiritual traditions on earth.

Tao (pronounced "dow") is often translated as "way" or "path." In one sentence, Tao is the intuitive search for reality, as well as that ultimate reality itself, and is distinguished by finding harmony in what appear to be opposites. China, with one of the world's oldest and most stable cultures, provided fertile ground for this path to evolve over many thousands of years. (The Chinese have had the time and peace to develop a thorough system, but just about every other native tradition has its own system of environmental energetics, or—as feng shui is often called in Europe—geomancy.) Feng shui is one of Taoism's most useful practices, with the power to invigorate the outer world in the same way that other Taoist work, such as acupuncture, t'ai ch'i, and shiatsu, can help the inner world. And because feng shui's principles are ageless, they adapt to any culture. This helps explain why it has recently gained a strong following in Europe and North America. Moreover, it meets the most important criterion of any healthful environmental practice: It works.

Feng shui can create environmental harmony with versatility, depth, and creativity, and affect our lives in many useful ways. We may use feng shui to realize any number of personal and communal goals, from the most mundane to the most universal, including:

- Making our home/office/personal environment more useful, happy, and revitalizing

- Clearing away clutter, blockages, and personal pitfalls in our spaces

- Giving us more vital energy to accomplish our goals

- Integrating our material goods and property more effectively into our larger lives

- Increasing the effectiveness, and thus the success, of our businesses

- Developing a strong, abiding intuition that senses new or hidden trends and forces

- Making us more attuned and sensitive to our environments, both local and global (feng shui was green millennia before the economy made "going green" so fashionable)

- Helping us understand the nature of the world and how to naturally be ourselves in it

Tao and Success

Beyond these specific achievements, feng shui can help us navigate our complete life path harmoniously and wisely. As Wen-Tzu, one of the early Taoist masters, wrote, "Personal success has nothing to do with ordering others, but is a matter of ordering oneself. Nobility has nothing to do with power and rank, but is a matter of self-realization. Attain self-realization and the whole world is found in the self. Happiness has nothing to do with outward wealth and status, but is a matter of inner harmony" (*Wen-Tzu*, Verse 4). So can feng shui really help us find this harmony at the root of success? Absolutely! Even though feng shui may seem to be only a branch of Taoism, it is a path where the part can lead to the benefits of the whole. While some of our goals will be reached in such an organic, easy way that the process will seem like magic, a real payment must be made through disciplined practice and focused hard work. At the same time, our own efforts aren't enough; we must be open to what the world gives us—and that interaction can be truly mind-changing. This movement and rest is yet another aspect of Tao. For those of us with an accepting attitude toward the world, finding harmony with Tao is a fine goal for one's life. Others of us may ask, Isn't there more to it than that? Then why not consider a marvelous question posed by Charles Dickens, once the world's most popular storyteller, in his own favorite novel, *David Copperfield:* What is necessary for you to become the hero of your own life? What better way to ask what it would take for our noblest goals and aspirations to become reality! Since many of us, and probably most when fully honest, do desire many of the material pleasures of life, let's look a bit more into the connection between inner harmony and outward comfort.

Feng Shui and Prosperity

We make a living by what we get. We make a life by what we give.

—Winston Churchill

Can we, and should we, use what began as a spiritual discipline to gain prosperity? Yes, if we sincerely grapple with three questions: What does prosperity mean *for me?* What do I owe in return for my prosperity? Where does money fit into all this? These are highly personal questions in which coming up with an answer is not as important as engaging in real self-reflection. Practicing feng shui is a two-way street; by working with our environment we also work on ourselves. We shouldn't mechanically follow this or that rule just because someone once said it was a rule. Rather, when we learn how our surroundings are interwoven with our lives, and discover what outer change can and cannot do, we also realize the state of our inner life and where we wish to go. The following short meditations can help us answer these three questions at the necessary level, that of our true self or essential being:

- What does prosperity mean *for me?* A pervasive cliché floating through some cultures holds that there is an unavoidable trade-off between wisdom and wealth, personal evolution and accumulation of resources, seeking the sacred and piling up cash. This idea has been expressed as: "Material poverty means spiritual riches, material riches mean spiritual poverty." For most people this is nonsense. Destitution necessarily confers neither nobility nor insight. Some of the most venal, malicious and destructive people have been dirt-poor—look at many of Flannery O'Connor's short stories about the greed and corruption of the poverty-stricken. Yes, someone can choose a path, like Saint Francis of Assisi, who felt it was necessary as a traveling priest living on charity to have no material possessions to encumber his work. On the other hand, individuals with great resources—from the emperors Ashoka (in India) and Antoninus (in Rome) to Andrew Carnegie and Bill Gates, to name but a few—have helped the poor, built schools and hospitals, fostered research, improved cities, and patronized the arts. The world is surely a better place because of them. Answering the prosperity question means finally asking ourselves, What do we really want? What do we already have in our life, and what are we doing with it? Feng shui really does begin at home.

- What are the obligations of prosperity? Most of us have many things in our lives for which to be thankful, while there are more than a billion people who are struggling every day and don't even have enough to eat. Isn't it selfish to seek additional prosperity for ourselves? Shouldn't we help our city, so hundreds or thousands have better lives? Shouldn't we help our country, so millions are more prosperous? Shouldn't we think of helping the planet first, so billions will be better off? Well, how does one get started in such widening circles of social consciousness and charitable action? Again, everything begins right here, with the cultivation of a virtuous self. Mahayana Buddhists vow to liberate every sentient being in the cosmos, but they must start with "waking up" themselves. Jesus of Nazareth said, (Matthew 7:4–5, RSV) "How can you say to your brother, 'Let me take the speck out of your eye,' when all the time there is a plank in your own? You hypocrite, first take the plank out of your own eye, and then you will see clearly to take the speck out of your brother's." Therefore, the inner work must always precede the outer. How can we make good with the wealth we have? Make ourselves Good.

- In practical terms, why isn't more money better than less? There's nothing unusual in imagining the benefits of more and more cash. The first thing to realize is that the getting and handling of money, especially when connected to feng shui, is never value-neutral. There is a universal principle called karma—the law of action and reaction—that's always at work. Karma holds, for example, that if you make money from a tobacco company stock, *you* will be harmed, because of those who are harmed by smoking the company's products. Modern science supports this idea: the late physicist David Böhm, among others, showed that in quantum physics everything is interconnected at the minutest levels. So we need to find a more insightful, more connected way of working and spending. Money, like everything else, is a form of energy, and feng shui is an effective tool to develop the clarity, will, and intuition to handle it beneficially. Someone living in a nurturing, harmonious environment will feel the necessity of dumping the tobacco stock and finding stock from a company that helps people, such as a clean energy, green engineering, or organic food company.[1] Someone creating a healthful, stimulating living space will discover what's healthful and stimulating in finances. It's not magic; it's another aspect of Tao. In the coming pages we'll learn, through the study of **ying/yang, ch'i,** and the **Five Elements,** how this comes about.

Using This Book—Outlines of The Path

One wonderful thing about feng shui is that you can begin practicing almost immediately, and helpful transformations show up quickly with the right attention and understanding. The basic principles of feng shui are simple. Success in feng shui comes from practically, creatively, and sensitively applying these principles in our own unique situations. So with our own environments, inner and outer, as our training ground, this book takes beginners through simple steps leading to an effective feng shui practice.

We start by learning some fundamental concepts

about Taoism, including its major expression as pairs of opposites, which are known traditionally as **Yin** and **Yang** (Chapter One). By harmonizing ourselves with these universal manifestations, we improve life energy, or vital force, which is called **ch'i** (Chapter Two). Enhancing this vital force is essential for feng shui and can lead to improved health and personal effectiveness, individual evolution, and true success. Enhancing ch'i also requires working with the **Five Elements**, which are patterns of change in both our environment and in ourselves (Chapter Three). We then see how the vital energy of a specific place can be improved (Chapter Four) and how patterns of change can work for our benefit outdoors (Chapter Five). Creating good indoor ch'i is featured next (Chapter Six), followed by, no surprise, using the Five Elements indoors (Chapter Seven). This plan of working with both life energy and patterns of change is deliberate: These two primary aspects of feng shui, ch'i, and the Five Elements are intimately related because all aspects of vital energy connect to patterns of change, and vice versa; ultimately there is just one world, one reality, which is the universal way, or Tao. Chapter Eight explores a few paths for the more experienced student, including keeping the virtues of being a beginner. Chapter Nine offers advanced material in the form of appendices.

How to Get the Most Out of the Book

Those of us eager to change our homes, our jobs, or any other aspect of our lives need to be patient. It's necessary to gain an intuitive understanding of the basic principles—Tao, ch'i, and the Five Elements—and see them in our lives before embarking on a plan for change. Feng shui is very precise in how it works with each individual, relating the inner environment to the outer. We need to understand where we're coming from in order to find a way to our goals. And because these goals are important, we must first discover, using these principles, our own unique requirements for well-being and personal success. One person's cure is another person's curse. Knowing that, we can then work accurately and precisely with the external environment, including sites of homes and businesses. Interesting environmental challenges and related events in life, like the usefulness of career change and how to best move homes or offices, will be explored. So even if you're wondering if your business could make more money or if that Ikea living room is really right for you, let's get on with this journey and see what turns up.

This book is an introductory presentation and is designed to be a workbook and guide to self-exploration. The essential work begins with the reader herself or himself. To that end, a warning: The temptation to use this new practice on our best friend or Aunt Maude should be resisted until more training and experience accumulates. The Law of Karma operates here as it does everywhere else, and inadvertently affecting someone else's energy in an unintended manner can have serious consequences. Feng shui is a way of working with fundamental energies that can be quite powerful, so it shouldn't be taken lightly or casually. Moreover, in trying to help others, we can inadvertently open ourselves to absorb some of their negative energy in unforeseen and unwanted ways. While many of us probably will get excited over what we can do with our new feng shui

knowledge, it's better not to make a show of it. Let the results speak for themselves. As Saint Francis of Assisi said, "Preach the Gospel whenever possible, and if necessary, use words."

Imagine getting a book on, say, Western music that only uses examples such as "Happy Birthday," commercial jingles, or the collected works of The Archies. In the world of human environments, buildings, and landscapes, we have the equivalent of Mozart and Miles Davis, and many of their creations have unmatched energy and harmony. The best examples are the best teachers, and we'll use them. Don't be intimidated when you see a reference to a building you've never heard of, built perhaps by some fellow named Louis Kahn. His Salk Institute, in La Jolla, California, shown on the left, mirroring the serenity and simple majesty of the Pacific and the sky behind it, functions as a practical and inspiring workspace, and is so in tune with its environment that its feng shui is extraordinary. In this digital age—and some may be reading this book digitally—tons of great photos, if not virtual tours, are a click away. So let's check out these great examples and try to sense and feel why they're so effective or so powerful. Who would take a music course without listening very carefully and attentively? As has been said many times, we get out of the work what we put into it.

On the other hand, it would be surprising if many of us haven't run across feng shui talks or read newspaper articles, picture books, or even desk calendars about feng shui. Some may have heard of areas, or "sectors," in rooms, such as the "money sector." Let's forget all of that here and start with a clean slate; thus any unnecessary baggage won't slow the learning process down. Nothing is truly known unless we've proved it to ourselves. As the mathematician Edmund Landau wrote at the beginning of one of the most influential primers ever written—*Foundations of Analysis*—"Please forget everything you have learned, because you haven't really learned it."

Reading is only the beginning of your educational opportunity here; the best learning occurs through doing. Feng shui is not just a form of knowledge; it's a practice, a way of doing; thus the best learning occurs actively, not passively. With this in mind, every chapter of this book offers a number of learning activities—stimulating and often fun things requiring at most paper, pen or pencil, and always our senses, our bodies, lots of imagination, and an open mind—to heighten our absorption and, importantly, insight into the subject. Knowing the words is like "talking the talk," but we need to be "walking the walk" for the path to become real.

Feng shui asks us to find a new gear, so to speak, in our way of sensing and interpreting the world. Such a discovery may not happen overnight, but patience will pay off; to this end the learning activities—called **Walking the Walk**—start simply and gradually stretch and enlarge our capacities in subtle and sometimes right-brained ways. Do them as regularly as feels bene-ficial; once the entire sequence has been practiced from

Chapters one through nine, going through them again will be at least as useful as the first time through: The activities will enrich you with new dimensions and colorations impossible before.

Some of these activities require jotting down observations and writing ideas, so a clean, dedicated notebook is a logistical necessity; moreover, looking back on earlier notes is both fun and enlightening.

Walking the Walk

There's a quotation from the great Taoist sage Lao Tsu that says that the journey of a thousand miles begins with one step. A more accurate translation is that a journey of a thousand miles begins with the ground beneath our feet, meaning that every action begins with nonaction, every movement with nonmovement. So it is here.

For feng shui this means we start all activities with a meditation to bring us more in touch with the totality of ourselves, as this effort is the key to finding that new way of working, that new gear in us. Sit in a comfortable, quiet place with a straight spine; ideally the hips are higher than the knees, so a heavy cushion on the floor is usually better than a chair. Try to relax the body as much as possible while maintaining good posture and deep, even breathing; try to sense every part of the body loosen up and release all tension. Then observe yourself just as you are at that moment in time. Don't suppress anything; let any feelings and thoughts manifest themselves. Just keep that little bit of conscious breathing room that lets you stay aware of yourself. The mind, being the mind, perhaps will chatter like a chased squirrel, so let it. The heart may feel light or heavy, so be it. Take it all in, just as it is. We'll see that this is a deeply Taoist activity, for all kinds of things are happening below the surface *about which we have no clue.* It may take ten minutes, or twenty, to notice the start of a new feeling of connection, something like a calm throughout the body coupled with a feeling of balance and sharp concentration without any distinct object of concentration. That's a huge achievement, actually, and certainly enough for the first activity! Moreover, this calm, relaxed, and open perceptiveness is the "square one" for most of the meditation exercises in this book, and indeed most of our feng shui activities. This frame of mind/body, which we will cultivate further in the coming sections, is analogous to the basic stance in t'ai ch'i, in which we simply try to stand properly. This is not as easy as people may think—some spend years practicing t'ai ch'i before they can do so properly! So give this exercise its due, and approach it seriously and respectfully. The rewards may be great indeed.

CHAPTER ONE

Taoism and the Roots of Feng Shui

*ao* is the hidden inner nature of everything, the ultimate character of the universe as a whole and the source of all separate and individual things. Moreover, it's not separate from us: Our search for Tao is also Tao. Tao is easily the most challenging concept we'll find here, in part because it's beyond conceptualization. Since it's both the foundation as well as the ultimate goal of feng shui, we'll try to ease into appreciating it bit by bit. At the same time, we must ponder these bits sincerely. Let's not be afraid to knock our head against the wall; flashes of insight and sudden, funny illuminations will invariably come. If we

keep pondering Tao and feel like the floor is slipping out from underneath us, we're on the right track!

The *Tao Te Ching* (pronounced "dow duh jing"), the ancient Chinese book of wisdom, is perhaps the most famous attempt to shed light on Tao. The title means "Book of the Way (Tao) and Its Virtue (Te)." The book, organized into eighty-one verses of varying length, was written around 500 B.C.E. by Lao Tsu, an older contemporary of Confucius, as a collection of wisdom that had been already present for millennia. In the very first line of the first verse we confront the inexpressible nature of the Tao: "The way that can be described is not the Eternal Way."[1] So what *can* anybody say about it?

Much like in the Gospel parables, Taoist writers use imagery, allusions, stories, and intuition-jolting paradoxes to get us "on the way," a phrase that itself describes one sense of Tao. Lao Tsu writes in Verse 4 of the *Tao Te Ching,* "Tao is empty, yet creating all things it is inexhaustible. Indeed an unfathomable abyss, it is the ancestor of all of us, the myriad creatures of this world." Although Tao can be "smaller and lower than dust," it is also infinitely immense and active in the sense of the Sioux word *Wakan*, meaning the most great and sacred power. Verse 25 of the *Tao Te Ching* says, "If you must picture Tao, see it as great—it makes heaven great, it makes the Earth great, it makes the true human being great. Mankind follows the laws of the Earth; the Earth follows the laws of Heaven; Heaven follows the law of Tao; but Tao follows only its own way." Now here's a critical point: Humans follow the "laws of the Earth," in the sense that we follow the laws of organic life on this planet, getting food, eating, sleeping, breeding, defending ourselves, and so on. But we also have a possibility of evolving and reaching higher, and if so we must search for the highest law, which is Tao. Realizing Tao is the final goal of feng shui. A few have made it, so let's take to heart the words of Jesus of Nazareth in the Gospel of Thomas (verses 80–82): "Let him who seeks, not cease seeking until he finds, and when he finds, he will be troubled, and when he has been troubled, he will marvel and he will reign over the All."

One additional aspect of Tao must be mentioned here, as it recurs often throughout the book. Most of us construct our opinions and ideas in terms of opposites, such as this is good, that's bad; income is up, overhead is down; the Tigers are hot, the Sox are cold. Such constructions can be useful, but there's a danger in seeing too much of an *either/or* nature to things. The world, as feng shui shows, is much more *both/and*, which is closer to Tao. As an exercise, try to sense this: The Earth is both dry and wet; the seasons are both hot and cold; the world is both matter and energy, both quality and quantity, both one single thing and infinitely divided. These realizations start to take us beyond another either/ or opposition to that of know/don't know. In practicing feng shui, remember that we always show something of both these conditions, knowing and not knowing, and neither of them as well; and searching for where we are at the moment is an important part of the path. Moreover, developing an intuition of what lies beyond opposites is the beginning of a deeper understanding.

There's a temptation that often arises when folks study Taoism to get too caught up in the words; what matters is what's behind the words—the wisdom that comes from doing, the understanding that comes through action. No less than the great psychologist Carl Jung warned that focusing on words, even the writings of a classic like the *Tao Te Ching,* without real experience of what motivates the words can lead to confusion or disappointment. So let's return to our actual practice, and feel the ideas come alive.

Walking the Walk

This can be a challenging exercise, but the rewards are significant. One benefit is that the right hemisphere of the brain becomes easier to access, a huge help in feng shui. To begin, as in the first practice (pages 17–18), sit in a comfortable position conducive to meditation. The inspiration for this exercise is the opening verse of the *Tao Te Ching:* "The Way that can be described is not the Eternal Way." Now try to sense your state of being without using words. Sounds easy? Not for most of us; we can barely bring our attention to, say, our left foot, and, before we know it, the word *foot* is stuck in the mind. Usually after even a moment of wordless awareness, phrases, sentence fragments, and verbal commentary intrude. Try to let this inner talk fade away of its own accord. See if you can go for longer and longer periods without inner conversation springing up. For some of us, recalling a piece of music is a helpful transition to the wordless state. Eventually this state will get very interesting. Can you sense, and even understand, something without assigning or relating a word to it? Most of us grasp the world through words, and if we can extend the *reach* of perception, we will grasp more of the world and in a different way. After a few sessions the exercise won't feel so strange, and there may be longer stretches of inner quiet and wordlessness.

The next step, literally, is then to try to experience the immediate environment in the same wordless state. Take a stroll through the home, office, and grounds at a time when there will be few interruptions. Try to sense or notice as much as possible but without using words. Don't try to conclude or decide anything. Just gather impressions. This exercise, the "wordless walk," will be a building block for much of the nitty-gritty exploration at the root of feng shui practice, so repeat it as many times as feels necessary to get a new take on the environment. There may be some surprising realizations. Like the trunk of a tree, this modest stroll, taking in everything from the low dust to towering cloud formations, will branch out into diverse and more specific exploratory practices in the coming chapters.

Returning to words, and reviewing some of our words about Tao, we've touched on the notion that there is an eventual unity behind opposites, such as whole-versus-part or same-versus-different. Peering through the other end of the lens, Tao creates diversity from unity by engendering contrasts or polarities. Everywhere we look, we can find some kind of opposite. For example, the chair in which we're sitting may feel hard to us if we compare it to a plush, overstuffed sofa. We could also compare the same chair to a concrete stoop and say that the chair feels soft in comparison. Lao Tsu comments: "Everyone in the world perceives beauty as beauty because there also exists ugliness; all know good as good because there is evil. Similarly, being and nothingness beget each other; easy and difficult complete each other; high and low support each other; sound and silence make music from each other; before and after circle each other eternally" (*Tao Te Ching*, 2). This tendency to find polarities everywhere is expressed in the Taoist concept of Yin/Yang. Because it's so fundamental, let's look at it in more detail.

Yin/Yang and Finding Harmony in Opposition

Many people find the most universal expression of Tao in the creation of opposites. They exist everywhere and in everything, such as high/low, hot/cold, hard/soft, light/dark (day/night), early/late, and so on. Yin/Yang is the expression of this universal tendency to form polarities. It's enlightening to look at the Chinese characters, or ideograms, for added insight into important words. Millennia ago, the ideograms began as literal "picture words" and are rich in symbols. The ideogram for Tao is marvelously suggestive and even esoteric: It shows the head of a sage with flowing hair and a foot raised as if to begin the dance of the magus, or shaman. It can also picture the foot of a bird brooding and quickening an egg. The ideogram for Yin derives from the image of a hillside shaded with passing clouds; the character for Yang also shows a hillside but this time with the Sun shining above pennants or banners waving in the wind. In fact the Sun is often called "The Great Yang." Yang is the tendency toward the bright, hard, hot, dry, and forceful, and its most general form is energy. So almost automatically we imagine Yin to be dark, soft, cold, wet, and yielding, with a general form of matter. But Yang and its complement, Yin, are never substances or specific things. They are a pattern of change, to and fro, back and forth, a dance of form. Yin is never alone, never without at least the seed of Yang; nor is Yang ever by itself—this is why we write "Yin/Yang" instead of "Yin *and* Yang." Nothing can ever be one hundred percent one or the other, for when Yang begins to dominate, Yin appears, and when Yin reaches a maximum, Yang reasserts itself. This is graphically shown in the t'ai ch'i symbol, seen everywhere from martial arts storefronts to the Korean flag.

While awareness of Yin/Yang may go back to prehistory, it's still relevant to what's happening today. As Albert Einstein discovered in the realm of physics, energy (expressed as Yang) and matter (expressed as Yin) are one, and transform themselves interchangeably. Our modern myth of creation begins with a "big bang" of pure energy.

T'ai Ch'i 陰 *Yin*

陽 *Yang*

Feng 風

Shui 水

氣 *Ch'i*

道 *Tao*

A Taoist would point out that space simultaneously had to become present to receive this energy and that space and matter-energy are ultimately one unity. And here WE are! As the ancient sages put it, Heaven must reach down to Earth, Earth must reach up to Heaven, and so the things of the world are born. Tao, Yin, and Yang form the triplicity of creation. In feng shui, working with ch'i and the Five Elements can also be seen as complementary opposites: The former looks into whole situations, while the latter looks at interrelated parts and divisions. Another way to pair off vital energy and patterns of change is the noun (Yin) and verb (Yang) relationship. So we can find the manifestation of Yin/Yang wherever we look, whenever we look, in the smallest and most ordinary of things to the grandeur of the cosmos.

Walking the Walk

Let's actively identify some the axes of Yin/Yang in the world around us, and in us. Strolling around the home and office, in no hurry and not preoccupied with anything, see how many different pairs of opposite qualities you can find. What's bright, and what's dark? What feels light, and what's heavy? Where are the materials hard, and where are they soft? Are some spots hot and others cold? Are some things new, some things old? (If this is beginning to sound like Dr. Seuss, good! Children can so often see so much better than adults.) There's no limit, in principle, to these pairings: One space can seem more urban, another one more rustic; one northeastern and one southwestern; one Mondrian and one Pollock. One homeowner in Maryland had been wondering why her place felt so uninviting, even though the furnishings and settings were of the highest quality, the house had the best workmanship, all of that. In one of these strolls it hit us: Every object was uniformly relatively large; nothing was particularly small or really big, like a grand piano or three-seat sofa. Even furniture showrooms typically display more variation in size. By creating different dimensional scales alone, this home became more interesting, more individualized—and the problem was solved.

And that's just the inside; on another occasion, go outside. What's permanent in the landscape, and what changes? If the day is cold and wet, wasn't it dry and sunny at some point earlier, and won't it be again? How did the transition take place, and did you catch the signals of transition? Note that, regardless of the season, what we perceive is relative to what's before and after; in the middle of July, 75 degrees can feel cool and refreshing, whereas in April such a temperature can feel scorching. Again we'll find the interplay of old and new, quick and slow, hard and soft, small and big, and so on.

You can also take in the workplace in this way. What's busy, what's quiet? Where are the areas of vital activity, and are there moribund spots? If so, notice whether things, even for a short stretch, become important or hurried, before getting drowsy again. You could look at specific projects at work and see how they expand and contract, get easy and then hard, move from a dynamic phase into a static period, and then change again. Conflict and resolution forms another pair that, while apparently opposite, feed into and create each other when the environment is healthy. There's an interesting work analogy to the Maryland home mentioned above: Ever see a business in which everyone has the same kind of personality? For example, there was a design firm on the West Coast in which everyone, even the IT guy, was an intensely outgoing bohemian. The company didn't last very long that way, with the conflict starting in the morning over which organic coffee was the most authentic. Without a play of opposites, no one can appreciate each other.

So the push-me/pull-you of Yin/Yang is everywhere; we can also find them in our own thoughts, feelings, and actions. And there's another learning experience!

CHAPTER TWO

Improving Ch'i and Increasing Life Energy

he *Nei Ching* ("Book of the Inner World"), a many-thousand-year-old Chinese medical treatise, says, "Yin/Yang is the Tao of Heaven and Earth. It is the common thread of everything ('the ten thousand things'); the father and mother of change and transformation; the beginning in which life and death are rooted" (Chapter 5). From the back-and-forth, to-and-fro movement of Yin/Yang comes vital energy, ch'i, the central concern and concept in feng shui. Verse 42 of *Tao Te Ching* says: "Tao gives birth to the one, the one gives birth to the two. The two gives birth to the three, and the three gives birth to everything. Everything descends to Yin and rises to Yang, and when this movement is balanced, ch'i brings harmony." This *ch'i* is often translated as "vital energy" or "life energy." It's pronounced "chee" as in cheese, especially when we "say cheese" for the camera: Smile, look alive! You may have heard of ch'i in the context of the martial arts, such as t'ai ch'i and karate; health and healing arts, such as shiatsu, ch'i kung, and acupuncture; as well as in sports and other physical contexts. That's because the movement of ch'i in the body is the basis for health and disease, strength and weakness. Similarly, the movement of ch'i in external space, such as on land and in water, in gardens and fields, and in the home and at work, is the basis for abundance and adversity. As with all living organisms, different forms of energy in the environment are always flowing and changing. So we'll learn how to align ourselves with good energy, avoid destructive energy, and adjust these currents in our personal spaces for optimum health and success. This process will be at the heart of our practice.

Indeed, creating good ch'i is the key to feng shui. A clear, comprehensive definition of ch'i, however, is likely to elude us until we've worked with it. And definitions themselves have built-in limitations: Is there one word in modern English that means intensity yet flexibility of mind, firmness yet suppleness of feeling, vigor and resilience of the body, wisdom and generosity of the spirit? If we were dwelling eight hundred years ago in south-central England, we could say that a person or place was hale, which comes from the word *whole* and means "healthy," words that at that time meant the same thing, and what we could point to as "good ch'i." Inevitably there's been a trade-off in our modern language between precision and scope, and we have nothing close to one word that captures ch'i these days. Its concept is cumulative, synergistic, and organic rather than reductionist, closed, and mechanical. So, as with many important concepts, ch'i is easy to understand once it clicks, but it's hard to summarize. So here's a great chance to work with our intuition, to accumulate a feeling for ch'i, and to refrain from overrationalizing.

Everything alive has its own ch'i; moreover, as Taoists see the world as alive, every individual and group of things has some kind of ch'i. "Life energy" merely begins to describe it, as it's not a quantity that can be measured in watts or horsepower. Rather, ch'i is a quality or kind of energy that promotes, develops, and advances. It is the kind of force that occurs when, to quote the late poet and author Guy Davenport, "every force evolves a form." It's the motivation behind patterns and organizations in the sense of organic structures, whether animal, vegetable, or mineral. Ch'i opposes disorder or loss of form (known as entropy). Refer again to the ideograms on page 29. The ideogram or character for ch'i shows a rice grain or seed, which for a Far Easterner is the source of life or "daily bread," giving off vapor, which rises to heaven and forms a cloud. This image is humble yet cosmic, like Tao itself, so we should consider it carefully.

It shows that ch'i is invisible, although essential, like the air. And, as vapor contains air and water, it summons us immediately to feng shui! This is because the words *feng shui* literally mean "wind water"—two of the most important, dynamic, and mysterious forces at work in our world. These two characters are also on page 29. Logically, feng shui emphasizes external and environmental kinds of ch'i, and these words further remind us that our goal is to humbly use and accommodate, not dominate and abuse. The wind can bring life-giving oxygen and moisture to a desert or smash a city in a hurricane. Can we tell the wind where to blow? Can we control an ocean current or river? Perhaps to some degree, but at what cost? Rather than control life energy, Taoism teaches us to intuitively understand and cultivate—work *with*—ch'i to achieve the harmony that brings lasting vitality.

The image of a cloud of vapor also connects to the idea of breathing, like our exhaling on a cold day. The Lakota chief Sitting Bull once said, "What is life? The breath of the buffalo on a winter morning." Everything alive—fish, trees, worms, cities, seas, cells—breathes one way or another. Many Taoists translate *ch'i* as "breaths," but their meaning is more embracing: breathing as a form of vibration, which is a movement in and out, back and forth, as in the ocean's tides. This fits their sense of a living universe, since every material substance or object vibrates, from atoms to stars like our Sun. Both physicists and philosophers have said that the world is made up of vibrations. As the *Nei Ching* says, "The deepest energies in the world are [these] breaths." The *Tao Te Ching* is certainly in agreement: "The universe is like a bellows, empty yet inexhaustible, moving and ever creating more and more" (Verse 5). The quote from Lao Tsu above (Verse 42) is so insightful and important that it bears repeating: When the movement between Yin and Yang is balanced, ch'i brings forth an abundance of creative power. Therein lies the major path ("tao" with a little *t*) in feng shui: balancing Yin and Yang to create healthy ch'i.

Let's look at some practical examples of ch'i. In the human body, when the right balance exists between Yin and Yang, that is, between activity and rest, work and play, thinking and sensing, the sacred and the profane, and so forth, we feel healthy, thoughtful, productive, and joyful. Human ch'i at its best shows us the best in humanity. A tree that has neither too much exposure nor too much shade, too hard nor too soft a soil, too much cold nor too much heat, thrives. The finest trees show the purest tree ch'i. Every community has its ch'i; the earliest feng shui masters strove to make towns and cities strong yet adaptable, safe yet sociable, orderly yet creative. Skilled workers and artisans intuitively know the ch'i of their subject. Notice how successful fishermen understand how different fish swim, feed, and migrate; understand air and water currents and other earthly forms of ch'i; understand nets, lines, boat handling, and a thousand other variable skills that constitute their own "fisherman ch'i." Performers such as athletes know all about ch'i. Notice how great actors not only get the body language, the speech, and the feelings of their subject but also find their characters' essence. How does a great mime become a cat? By mimicking the sinuous, balanced movements, the dispassionate stare, the relaxed but predatory grace, and all the other hallmarks of "cat ch'i."

Walking the Walk

The best place to begin to understand ch'i is within oneself. Not enough vital energy and we die, whereas abundant ch'i brings energy, wisdom, and accomplishment. Yet even too much ch'i is a kind of imbalance and can cause health problems, although this is an extraordinarily rare situation. There is a story of a Taoist master in China more than one hundred years ago who perfected the art of concentrating ch'i in the body; carried away with the success of his work, he didn't stop until he physically exploded. Whether true or not, the story provides a good metaphor. For most of us, to be good at feng shui, as with anything else, we need to improve our ch'i. Here are three great ways to walk that path:

- A classic exercise is the Great Cycle meditation: Sit in a quiet, undisturbed place with the knees below the hips and the spine straight. Relax and let thoughts and feelings subside. Concentrate on the area at the base of the spine and gradually imagine that it's warming up. You can even imagine that there's a source of light radiating from that spot. Then, with no hurry or pushing, imagine the heat—actually try to feel it—rising up through the center of the spine and radiating throughout the back. Let the warmth continue rising through the back of the neck to the base of the skull and then slowly, pleasantly arcing over the top of the head until it reaches the forehead. Imagine the heat continuing down the center line of the front of the body, passing between the eyes, behind the nose, behind the back of the mouth and tongue (it also helps to keep the tip of the tongue in contact with the back of the upper teeth during this exercise), and down the throat. Feel the heat continue down through the chest, behind the solar plexus, past the stomach, and into the belly. The area a few inches below the navel is a reservoir of ch'i, called the *tan t'ien* in Chinese and the *hara* in Japanese (and indeed, the ritual suicide of opening the hara is called hara-kiri, or seppuku), so let the warmth and light collect in this area before it sinks back to the base of the spine. Then repeat the cycle at least a few times until the body feels suffused with a pleasant warmth. In contrast to most activities in our fast-food sound-bite culture, the slower this exercise is done the better. The more detail the imagination can connect to, for example, "The left shoulder blade now feels warm, now the right, and now the back of the neck," and so forth, the better. We need to take our time, for most of us don't really know our bodies.

There's great benefit to doing ch'i-building exercises under the eye of a master and with the social energy of a class, and most communities have schools offering t'ai ch'i ch'uan and ch'i kung. T'ai ch'i ch'uan (pronounced "tie jee chwan") is an ancient Chinese discipline of meditative movements usually combined into martial arts forms; ch'i kung (pronounced "chee gung") is an equally ancient series of postures and movements that stimulate the flow of ch'i in the body. Every intensive feng shui study involves one or both of these activities. However, there's a lot we can do on our own (and some helpful books are listed in the bibliography). One of the

all-time best strength and
energy builders is the Circle
Stance exercise (recall that
life energy naturally circles):

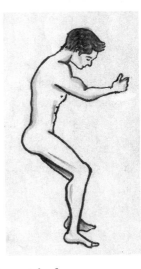

- Get a large exercise
  ball (use one at the
  gym, borrow one from
  a friend, or, better
  yet, buy your own, for
  many types of exercises
  can be done with it):
  a thirty-inch version is about right for someone
  five-ten or taller; shorter people can use a slightly
  smaller ball. Place the ball between the legs with
  the feet a little more than shoulder-width apart,
  and gently and lightly sit on it. Point the toes
  straight ahead; it's not unusual to feel moderate
  pressure on the outside of the lower leg. Feel the
  body's position precisely and remember it. Then,
  using that sphere-outlining stance, hold the ball
  to the chest with the arms around the equator,
  and conform the torso to the ball, hips below and
  shoulders above. Feel the body's position precisely

and remember it. Then lose the ball and hold that exact position from three to ten minutes, not more than once a day. Make sure to breathe abdominally, taking in relaxed, deep belly-breaths. The joints and muscles should feel as relaxed as possible, even though this is real work, especially keeping the head, jaw, and neck loose, with a free-floating feeling. It's okay to use the ball again now and then to perfect the posture. An important note: If the knees are a little beat-up or get sore on you, back off from the exercise in either duration or frequency—learning to listen to our bodies is a huge step forward in this work.

• While special exercises are great, Taoist masters used everyday activities to boost vital energy. Everyone breathes, but a master takes the deepest, slowest, and most relaxed breaths; everyone eats, but a master chews very slowly and deliberately, savoring every bit of food (and eats far less than most people, although the quality is much higher); everyone sleeps, but a master rests as much as necessary to get up completely refreshed and revitalized.

The amount of vital energy wasted through tension, unnecessary exertions, and inefficient work is astounding. Let's try a few of these "relax!" reminders each day; the results will be stunning.

When dealing with a more serious energy imbalance or blockage, shiatsu and acupuncture can have a powerfully tonic effect—by all means see an expert. Both shiatsu and acupuncture stimulate the body's own "power lines" of ch'i, called meridians, shiatsu by touch and acupuncture by tiny needles. These meridians have different qualities and functions, usually related to the Five Elements, mentioned earlier. It's good to understand these energy flows and qualities because a great deal of what an acupuncturist does to harmonize ch'i inside the body parallels what a feng shui practitioner does in the outer environment. As Nili Portugali, an Israeli architect and teacher, has observed:

> In any organic system, each element has its own uniqueness and power, but always acts as part of a larger entity to which it belongs and which it complements. Having adopted

this concept, I do not regard urban design, architecture, interior design, and landscape design as independent disciplines removed from each other, but as one continuous and dynamic system.[1]

We can go a step further and regard all environments and their associated life energies as connected, changing systems. Just as cities have their own ch'i, so do buildings, houses, and individual rooms. Sometimes it's obvious what we like or don't like about these spaces; other times there's only a vague feeling. We can all remember visiting a place where, regardless of our activity there, we felt refreshed and invigorated. Conversely, we may have felt drained, irritated, or sad for no other obvious reason. Imagine having to live in the latter place as opposed to the former! Because the ch'i of most places on Earth can be adjusted for the better, every human civilization and culture has its own form of feng shui. In the West in recent times it's most often called geomancy. Regardless of the name, the main concern the world over in this science/art has been to cultivate good ch'i. While there isn't a pat formula for it, the beginning feng shui practitioner needs to first get a feel for the different kinds of ch'i that affect homes, offices, and other kinds of spaces. Then we can synthesize all our impressions and "vibes" into an intuitive sense of the whole space. Only then should we consider what changes are possible. And, as good physicians must remind themselves, we do no harm. Adjusting ch'i is a careful, subtle process because of all the levels of activity, the personal and interpersonal dynamics, aspirations, memories, economic considerations, and more that are involved. A room, as psychologists know, is never just a room. Feng shui can be said to know that even better. So let us begin exploring the specific kinds of ch'i we'll be working with. We'll begin with general, even worldwide, kinds of ch'i before moving to the specific. Then we'll begin to see the ways in which ch'i can be adjusted for the better.

Environmental Ch'i

For a single planet, Earth has a fantastic range of natural environments! Each of these ecosystems nurtures unique forms of life, varying even among neighboring jungles or tundra, deserts, plains, and so on. In a similar way, people live differently in Maine, Miami,

New Mexico, and Minneapolis. It's a shame, by the way, that grade schools no longer make geography a required study; what better way to appreciate the diversity of our world than to pore over a kaleidoscopic panoply of mapped-out places, things, and peoples? On the largest scale, the flow of the Sun's energy (and not just the light in a human's visible range) bathing the Earth influences every local ch'i. Environmental light is a significant factor in feng shui, and an entire book could be written on light and ch'i; here we begin with this commonsense question: How will the Sun shine on a site or building through the yearly cycle? Another related large-scale factor is climate. Does it vary wildly, as in Chicago, which endures winter plunges to 50 degrees below zero (with wind chill) and in summer steams in frequent 100-degree humidity? Or is it generally stable, like Los Angeles, which always seems locked between a fairly dry 55 and 85 degrees? Is the site overly exposed to wind or harsh elements? Near a large or small body of water? Is there a rainy and dry season? Knowledge of these conditions helps us to live efficiently and harmoniously, without pointless waste. Essentially practical, feng shui demands seeing the obvious and developing good common sense. Examples of the complete lack of such are all around us: It's amazing that in the American West, homes continue to be built surrounded by scrub grasslands that periodically get so dry that large, widespread fires are inevitable. Another disaster in the offing is the national trend to live right on an exposed seacoast: In the East, increasingly frequent and more powerful hurricanes make many unbuffered coastal zones dangerous places to dwell.[2] On that topic, it seems obvious that humans are having an effect on the Earth's climate, such as the very visible melting of the polar ice cap and countless glaciers, so we'll see that on many levels feng shui can help us "green" our lives and help the planet.

Environmental ch'i includes many smaller and subtler factors, and even hidden ones. We need to notice the quality of the soil: Is it too rocky, shallow, densely clayed, or polluted? How is the drainage? Where is the water table? Notice which plants thrive and which ones don't in and around the site you're interested in. Are there animals, and how do they interact with the site, and its humans, if at all? What else is in the neighborhood—homes, offices, factories, shops, or highways? As said before, we must use all of our five senses in detecting ch'i. But what about the hidden sources of ch'i? These could be anything from buried cables to underground streams, from low levels of radioactivity to angles on a neighboring building. Hidden ch'i can often have major effects, good or bad, on the occupants of a site, and so we'll learn ways of detecting hidden ch'i.

An extremely important part of the energy that surrounds us, often the strongest of all, comes from other people. Feng shui traditionally takes for granted that our parents, partners, children, relatives, friends, and coworkers are all fixed in the firmament of our lives and shouldn't be "adjusted" even if they could be. However, modern America is more mobile and socially elastic than any traditional society could have imagined; what seemed unimaginable in eighteenth-century Beijing, such as a no-fault divorce, is just one visit to a court clerk in twenty-first-century Boston. As human ch'i evolves new forms, feng shui must keep up, so we'll take a look at evaluating these energies in our environment. In addition, we'll see that there are established practices of studying and improving relations between us and our neighbors and even between us and our predecessors and successors in the home and at work.

Walking the Walk

Pick a town (and you can do this more than once) or city with which you're familiar or willing to explore and study. Using the ideas of the preceding section, figure out how the natural setting influenced the town's layout, orientation, construction, appearance, and overall character, especially its human activities, and how, when, and why they take place. Was the presence of a river the reason for the city's founding? Was it nearby mines? How do light, wind, and weather affect the buildings throughout the year? How do seasonal changes affect activities? For two extreme examples, consider Aspen and Daytona Beach. Think of people who embody the character or unique energy of these locales. Optional exercise: Run through this again with a favorite place in the country or a wilderness area and consider the plants and animals (flora and fauna) and how they fit within their natural setting.

Dangerous Ch'i

Most kinds of ch'i, when they are not in unnatural overabundance, are not intrinsically harmful to people.

But there are types of ch'i that are simply bad for us. Traditional Chinese practitioners call them *hsia* (pronounced "shah") *ch'i,* meaning "killing ch'i," and *hsieh* (pronounced "sheh") *ch'i,* meaning "perverse ch'i." Living next to a hospital could be disastrous because of the all the negative vibrations of illness and death one would be exposed to; the same goes for living next to a funeral home, mortuary, or slaughterhouse because of the sheer amount of death in the immediate atmosphere. Just one horrific event sometimes can change the ch'i of a place for a long time. A midwestern teacher and her family moved into a home in which a notorious and particularly grisly murder had taken place years before. Although many purification rituals, both Western and Eastern, had been used on the house since the murder, the husband fell into poor health and eventually died before his time. Was the cause of his ill health *hsia ch'i* or was it genetic, dietary, work-related, or psychological? Let's reframe the question, because the world is more "both/and" than "either/or." The cause could be any combination things, so why take chances? The new owners didn't; they had the house demolished so they could build afresh. While some kinds of harmful ch'i are universally noxious—no one should live next to a fetid swamp, for example—other effects depend on the individual. A recovering alcoholic shouldn't be exposed to bar or tavern ch'i, nor should a vegan live near a ranch or livestock farm.

Sensing and understanding the ch'i of a place is only the first step in the art of energetic adjustment; if some kind of change is needed, what are the general principles of these adjustments?

Improving Vital Energy: The Long View

Ch'i in our personal and work spaces is rarely so elevated and strong that it can't be enhanced. Based on what we've just learned, there are three simple goals in adjusting ch'i. In one-word summaries, these goals are *balance, flow,* and *authenticity.*

- *Balance:* As the *Tao Te Ching* states, life energy comes from the right balance between Yin/Yang. Good ch'i in a space comes from balancing opposites of light, color, movement, textures, shapes, perceptions, feelings, functions, and a myriad of other quantities and qualities, whether changing in time or (for a while at least) frozen in the space itself. Sometimes it will be easy to adjust these things, sometimes not. The largest kinds of ch'i, like the climate and geography, may seem impossible to change, and on the surface that might be true. For example, if someone loves dry weather and lives in Seattle, what can she do but move? Or what does a person do if he loves the shore and lives in the mountains? The answer is plenty, at least in terms of indoor space. The person living in the hills won't be able to go outside and stroll along the beach, but it's possible to make, say, his work area powerfully connect with many of the positive energies found at the seaside. The Seattle dweller can make her living room feel like the Sonoran Desert. With the right feeling for balance, there's no Yin that can't be made more Yang or vice versa. Our new sensitivity to ch'i will then tell us what's too little or too much. This feeling for balance is as old as human philosophy itself; the ancient Greeks spoke emphatically of seeking the "Golden Mean," while the followers of Confucius collected many of his teachings in "The Doctrine of the Mean," one of the pillars of traditional Asian wisdom.

Thus we will be returning to the question of balance throughout the coming sections.

• *Flow:* It's in the fundamental nature of ch'i that it must *flow.* Energy, as in life energy, must move around and change. Barriers, blockages, bottlenecks, obstructions, and gummy spots are the bane of relaxed, easy-flowing ch'i. Air that doesn't move turns stale and stagnant; water becomes foul—back to "wind and water" again! Yet just about anything else can stagnate: furniture styles, photos, equipment, plants, and partners. As the goal of the acupuncturist is to eliminate congestion in the flow of the energy pathways of the body, so will the feng shui practitioner eliminate congestion in environmental ch'i. Clutter in a room, for example, is often a huge problem for healthy ch'i. Many people have noticed that well-to-do Victorians, with their love of overstuffed living spaces, suffered from a rich kind of intellectual, emotional, and spiritual congestion. The nineteenth-century American author Henry Adams, for example, who had an acute understanding of the connection between environment and disposition, notes in his autobiography, "The (bourgeois) English mind was like the English drawing room: a comfortable and easy spot, filled with bits and fragments of incoherent furnitures, which were never meant to go together, and could be arranged in any relation without making a whole." Zing! However, before anyone throws stones . . .

The other side of the clutter coin is a problem, too, when ch'i flows too quickly in a space—another reason why we stress the importance of balance first. Now we must slow down the ch'i and prevent it from leaving too quickly. For example, is there too much change, too much turnover, in our decor, or in our work, or in our life? There is a very American habit of always wanting the latest thing or the new, improved version, and rushing like mad to get it. Does our home ever make us want to stop and smell its roses, so to speak, or do we always run to get out? Flow is good, but moderation is a virtue in the movement of ch'i, as it is in life itself.

- *Authenticity*: A sow's ear will never be a silk purse, so let's not fool ourselves that it is or someday might be. Plastic furniture is not wood furniture, no matter how cleverly it's disguised; feel it, smell it, knock on it and listen, and see if we're fooled. Better to let plastic be what it is and shine forth in all its iridescent, chemically colored glory: a petroleum product that, like oil, is shiny and homogeneous and at the same time hard. In the human realm, success means being one's true self. On a different scale, consider the business fortune of Starbucks: Having lost the ch'i of an authentic neighborhood café during a period of rapid growth, the stock of Starbucks soon dropped more than 50 percent in value. Granted, all things change over time, but if we really appreciate something, why hide its age? Weathered gray shingles on a Cape Cod house can be more interesting and aesthetically compelling than the same home with yet another coat of white paint. Authenticity is also important in terms of function. A bathroom is not a library, unless our reading material has the character of cleaning and waste removal (unlikely). It's not a good idea to do much of our work in the bedroom because a good bedroom has the ch'i of rest and recuperation, not effort, concentration, and discipline. As we'll see later, libraries present problems for working, too. Neither is it wise to try to sleep in one's office. Authentic ch'i is especially good to consider in terms of interior design. What does copying a certain style really mean? What does it say about the owner? For example, a family of Central and Eastern European ethnicity hired a decorator who favored Mediterranean styles, such as Italian chairs and Spanish lamps. In the course of time, the family added pictures, ceramics, and textiles from their own heritage; eventually their living room felt like the environmental equivalent of a bowl of paella goulash.

An important realization in the work of generating good ch'i is that we should practice moderation in moderation, meaning there are situations when extremes are needed. Perverse (*hsieh*) and deadly (*sha*) ch'i and all other harmful kinds of ch'i simply must be eliminated. Even though there can be a huge range in the degree of danger, show no mercy, whether it means eliminating jarring decor, bare earth on the property, dead houseplants or trees, dust bunnies, vermin, trip cords, structural weak-nesses, or leaking gas lines. It's amazing what people can get accustomed to and no longer see as a threat. The use of chamber pots in premodern Europe and the dumping of the vessels' contents just outside the house had an impor-tant connection to the occupants' low life expectancy and frequent ill health, not to mention death from plagues! Toys left on the lawn are nowhere near as noxious, yet they do affect the ch'i of the home, and who wants to risk a lawsuit when someone trips over them?

Walking the Walk

Make an inventory of the ch'i in your immediate envi-ronment. What's the energy like in the room you're read-ing in? Does it feel sedate, off-kilter, or bustling? What is the main source of that feeling—a bed, a bookcase, a fireplace, or a view? What about the whole house or office ch'i? Take a moment to walk around and simply attend to the energy; assume nothing and use "fresh" senses, like a child's eye seeing something for the first time. Look for imbalances among those oppositions we've seen earlier: Are things too open or too cluttered, too hard or too soft, too bright or too dull, too busy, too inactive, and so on. The more details you notice the better. See how these opposing qualities interact. Try to see movement and change on a different time scale: Will that pile of papers be there tomorrow or next week? Is that shelf or this arrangement of chairs ever going to be different? Who or what will change them? Do the same thought experiments outside. Include in your questions the following: What is the ch'i of the physical environment in the neighborhood? Are plants flourishing? Is the air pleasant or unpleasant? Is there water nearby, and what is its quality? Are there many people, and are they predominately young or old? What about the whole town, village, or city? What's the character of the surrounding countryside? Write it all down in the notebook. We are often surprised at what we notice when we let our thoughts and feelings roam around freely.

Here's an interesting little exercise to see if personal ch'i is moving too fast: Most of us can't function without a wristwatch, which says something right there. For one day, keep your watch in a pocket (one clever person hid it in his sock) so that every time it has to be checked, there's a conscious reminder that you are conforming to some schedule. Try to count how many times you reach in your pocket (or discreetly look at your sock). How do you feel about this?

As opposing tendencies (Yin/Yang) are found in everything, so we will find them in learning to harmonize our environment. As noted earlier, work with vital energy tends to be holistic; on the other hand, we'll need to look at interrelated and evolving parts to have more success improving the whole. Knowing these constituent elements gives us an understanding of environmental materials, both raw and finished, and how they influence our lives. The substances found in our living and work spaces, like steel, wood, plaster, cloth, plastic, glass, and so on, and how they're shaped and how they're used, have fascinating and deep connections to our health, moods, ideas, activities, friendships, and bank accounts—and vice versa. Whether the system is a company, a house, or the human body, there will be predictable patterns of change among these parts. Let's look at these patterns, which is the study of the Five Elements and their use in feng shui.

CHAPTER THREE

The Five Elements
and Natural Patterns
of Change

re there people, places, and things in a business that work smoothly and effortlessly together? Are there rooms in the house where the furnishings and contents don't seem happy together? Do natural or urban settings have buildings that fit in beautifully or stick out like sore thumbs? Is there an activity or energy in a room that's great for one person and not so great for another? What are some of the tricks top designers use to blend seemingly incongruous objects to express something special for their clients? Working with the Five Elements gives us insight into these and other environmental patterns. This work is not a

shifting of gears from the previous chapter; in actuality we're continuing and extending the task of creating good ch'i. The Five Elements manifest aspects of Yin/Yang just like everything else, and when we harmonize them, good energy results. So here we get a new, highly effective set of tools to create good ch'i.

The Five Elements in traditional Chinese science are wood, fire, earth, metal, and water. These names are symbols, not actual substances, and as symbols they are appropriately flexible. For example, a building that has a fire nature, like a church, a chemical factory, or a Gothic Revival house, has a symbolic, not physical, connection to what happens when we light a match. So "element" does not mean something static and fixed, like "the element helium." The word *elemental* more closely suggests primal simplicity. The Five Elements are not like atoms, which are fairly indestructible, microscopic building blocks, but more like steps in a process. They're not even limited to concrete materials, such as the wood of a chair, which may have an earth or metal affiliation in its design. The Five Elements are more like a pattern of how substances form and change, where one element is inconceivable without its relations to the other four.

Indeed, the legendary Taoist sage Fu Hsi didn't call them elements at all, naming them instead "five stages of change" *(wu hsing* in Chinese). Sometimes we'll follow his lead and, stressing some of their important characteristics, call them growth (wood), transformation (fire), preservation (earth), discrimination (metal), and dissolution (water). Although these descriptions lack the sensual, poetic immediacy of wood, fire, earth, metal, and water, they help us to see the parts of a continually changing system where one element furthers or retards another. Dissolution promotes growth; growth promotes transformation; transformation promotes preservation; preservation promotes discrimination; and discrimination promotes dissolution, starting the cycle anew. In contrast, growth hinders preservation; preservation hinders dissolution; dissolution hinders transformation; transformation hinders discrimination; and discrimination hinders growth, starting this cycle again. Thus the elements constantly mutate into and influence one another, through two different cycles: one that advances and another that restrains. Whether we use one term or another (and we'll use both sets), the important thing is to have an intuitive and perceptual grounding that sees this pattern constantly at work in the world.

One reason the traditional names of the Five Elements have endured for several thousand years is the natural ease in visualizing their transformations in the two cycles. In the creative cycle, *wood creates fire*, as literal wood feeds a fire on a hearth or in a stove; as fire leaves ash, *fire creates earth;* as metals are found in the earth, *earth creates metal;* in turn *metal creates water,* as when real metal promotes condensation or becomes like quicksilver; as trees need water to grow, *water creates wood;* and so the cycle begins again. In the destructive cycle, *wood destroys earth*—imagine tree roots splitting the ground and absorbing soil; *earth destroys water*—as when earth muddies water (think of a swamp); *water destroys fire*—as water puts out fire; *fire destroys metal*—as fire melts metal in a furnace; *metal destroys wood*—as a metal ax cuts wood; and the cycle begins again. (See the diagram on the next page.) Notice that through the two cycles, each element is connected to the other four.

The best way to learn the Five Elements is to work the imagination, connecting rational thoughts with intuition, images, and symbols. Try to let their relations unfold as you notice these elements in rooms, in buildings, in the landscape, and in ourselves and other people. An excellent way to learn about each element, since it's a symbol for a phase or part of a cycle, is through its many connections to other natural cycles, like those of the seasons, the time of day, the weather, and the five visible planets. Indeed, our world is built of cycles, from the chemical cartwheels found inside living cells to the dance of galaxies. Some will ask, How do the five visible planets form a cycle? Remember that they're symbols, too; during most of human history the planets

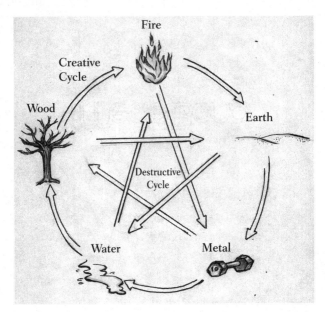

represented deities who governed movement in the cosmos, so their connection to the Five Elements is instructive and deep. (If you have an interest in astrology, you'll discover additional levels of connection; although these are beyond the scope of this book, resources for further study are listed in the bibliography.)

Summary of the Five Elements and Their Dynamics

- *Wood* symbolizes things that grow, create, and generally expand themselves. Elemental wood is anything sprouting, building, transforming into structure, and, like many trees or plants, it is tall and slender, long-grained, and stringy. Wood is affiliated with the spring season; its colors are green and green-blue, and its direction is east. Its time of day is morning. Its planetary affinity is with Jupiter. The higher virtues of wood are generosity, dedication, and mercy. Wood is fed by water and in turn feeds fire in the creative cycle; it breaks down and depletes earth and is cut by metal in the destructive cycle.

- *Fire* symbolizes things that enlighten, transform, inspire, heat, consume, cling, speed up,
  rise or explode as well as anything like tongues of
  flame—forked, sharp, leaping upward, intense;
  elemental fire also rules chemical transformation. Fire is affiliated with summer; its colors are
  red and orange, and its direction is south. Fire's
  time is midday, and its planetary manifestation is
  Mars. The higher virtues of fire are inspiration,
  action, and reason. Fire is fed by wood and itself
  feeds earth (creation cycle); fire melts metal and
  is quenched by water (destruction cycle).

- *Earth* symbolizes stability, firmness without hardness, nurturing, storing, and resilience. Earth forms
  are level, flat, low, grainy, gentle, and smooth,
  never more than a little irregular. Earth colors
  are yellow, tan, and brown; its direction is the
  center, and its season is the late summer. Its time
  of day is afternoon. Its planetary affinity is with
  Saturn. The higher virtues of earth are restraint,
  conservation, and faith. Earth is created by fire
  and in turn creates metal in the creative cycle; it
  destroys water (as when it turns into mud) and in

turn is destroyed by wood (as when wood absorbs earth) in the destructive cycle.

- *Metal* symbolizes contraction, density, hardness, smoothing and rounding, and cooling. Metal forms are hard, circular, and solid, like coins. Metal colors are white, silver, and pale gold; its direction is west. Metal's season is fall, and its time of day is evening; its planetary affinity is with Venus. The higher virtues of metal are justice, righteousness, and purity. Metal is made from earth and in turn liquefies into water in the creative cycle; metal cuts wood and is itself melted by fire in the destructive cycle.

- *Water* symbolizes anything that flows, cools, spreads, seeps, submerges, and dampens. It's alternately wavy, serpentine, and swirling, or formless, taking the shape of its container. Its colors are black, deep blue, and violet; its direction is north. Water is connected to the winter season; its time of day is late night, and its planetary affinity is with Mercury. The higher virtues of water are wisdom, mystery, and intuition.

Water is produced from metal and in turn feeds wood in the creative cycle; it quenches fire and is muddied by earth in the destructive cycle.

While this list may seem rich in associations, it only scratches the surface of the Five Element system; people who use the elements, such as acupuncturists and herbologists, study them their whole lives. Nevertheless, whether we're experts or beginners, our goals are the same as when working with ch'i: to strive for balance, flow, and authenticity. Recall that balancing ch'i means finding the right equilibrium between creating too much and too little vital energy; balancing the Five Elements means encouraging each element to express itself without excess or deficiency. The healthy movement of both the creative and the destructive cycles is needed to create and maintain this harmony—the need, again, to have the right proportion of Yang and Yin. What's more, *we,* living and working in various places, are a big factor in what elements are there and how they interact. Thus we need to see how the Five Elements appear not only in our environment but also in ourselves.

The Five Elements in Us

We've all seen it: an office that energizes and focuses one person will tire and distract another. A house that brings comfort and serenity to one person will drive another person crazy. Whoever is living and working in a given environment is a crucial part of the elemental balance and must be given first priority in any feng shui work. And every one of us has some combination of the Five Elements at work in our thoughts, feelings, and actions. Even though the elements are always in a process of transformation, most people gravitate toward expressing one of the five in their character; moreover, our physical bodies lean toward one element or another, and usually do so for life. This combination of physical, mental, and emotional traits is called one's type, and to know it has been a goal of countless systems of self-knowledge—astrology, constitutional psychology, numerology, and personality studies, to name a few—since time began. And for good reason; what you are and what you need are inextricably connected. The following is a list to help us learn more about ourselves in relation to the Five Elements. Rarely does anyone express just one element all the time and in all parts of life; most of us mix one dominant quality with one or more of the others. All of us have at least some of each element in our constitution. Again, a balanced amount is the goal with any element, in a person as well as in the environment. Too much of one element and we're off-kilter; too little and we also suffer. Finally, as was said in the introduction, resist the temptation to tell friends and relatives that they are, for example, a "typical water type." We need to observe, scrutinize, and study people wholeheartedly, yet keep our thoughts to ourselves.

- The **Wood** Person: Do you know somebody who's usually driven by goals; who's expansive, broadminded, and growth-oriented; who's creative and often buried in work? This person has a lot of the wood element in his or her makeup. Physically, wood-dominated folks tend to be tall and are often thin; they will be well built and have good muscle tone when in balance but when imbalanced can look like a gnarled tree or a willow wand. Wood people like to feel that they're on a mission or a quest, and their emotional life is organized behind their goals. They're also demonstrative and generous, and, if they're careful not to deplete themselves, a broad perspective complements their well-focused energy. Yeah, but don't tell an intensely wood person to "stop"—it literally goes against their grain. Mentally, they're tolerant and creative and take initiative. They favor large gestures and have good vision, in all senses of the word. In a tough situation they can bend but not break. Deficiency in the wood element leads to weak musculature, depression, lack of opinions, and being easily swayed—a "floating weed," as what many Far Easterners call it: someone whom the currents of life carry along wherever they go. Excess wood is seen in a tendency to anger, in stubbornness, prejudice, gluttony, delusions, grandiosity, and highly opinionated, empty rhetoric. Sometimes these folks are like overly big trees: stuck in their ways, inflexible, oblivious of others, and ripe for a storm to knock down. Wood people like sour foods and windy weather, and they should watch out for liver or gallbladder problems.

Wood professions and activities: architecture, composition, construction, executive or administrative work, farming and horticulture, growth industries, noninvasive and herbal medicine, novelties, painting, and travel-related work.

- The **Fire** Person: Do you know someone charismatic, energetic, and action-oriented who's a force for transformation and change? That individual has lots of the fire element. Typically the fire person looks ruddy, wiry, and compact; he or she is agile, quick, and sharp in movement. Fire people are emotionally confident, optimistic, cheerful, and often volatile but tend toward joy and warm-heartedness. They love to love, ardently, and to be loved, emphasizing the transformative powers of romance. When fire is well balanced in the mental world, fire people are inspired, tenacious, insightful, acute, incisive, and leaders by temperament. They speak well, if sharply, at times and may be gifted with language ability. Deficiency in fire leads to sluggishness, dullness, meekness or lack of self-assertion, holding grudges, and a clichéd or weak mind. Excess fire leads to explosive moods, violence, mania, giddiness, and trouble-making of the most foolishly idealistic sort (as in the road to Hell is paved with good intentions).

Fire people like hot weather and bitter foods; the fire-affiliated parts of the body are the heart (including the blood and circulatory system) and small intestine.

Fire professions and activities: chemical engineering, cooking, leatherwork, ministry and preaching, surgery, teaching (less the facts and more the spirit), veterinary medicine, and animal husbandry.

- The **Earth** Person: Often we know but don't always recognize someone with a lot of the earth element: a conservative, quiet, practical person who is often devoted to preserving and taking care of things and who, in a nonflashy (meaning less fire), nonexpansive (less wood) way, accomplishes substantial tasks over time. Such a person's motto might be "Slow and steady wins the race." The shop that will have that one piece of hardware, that one book, that one new color, is often run by an earth type.

  Earth individuals are fleshy, solid, deliberate in movement, often built "low to the ground"; they are emotionally calm, honest, sympathetic, trusting, and mentally pragmatic; their thinking is durable, focused, and helpful. Earth people can be ambitious to accumulate something or "succeed" in material ways; they can also be devoted and considerate helpmeets. Stability and family of some kind, which could mean a business, are central to them. Excess earth is seen in selfishness, hard-heartedness, rudeness, crudeness, and a manipulative quality. Deficiency in earth is seen in reflexive selflessness, extreme sacrifice or asceticism, worry, gloominess, and negativity. Strong earth types like a humid climate and sweet foods, and they should watch their stomach and spleen.

Earth professions and activities: preservation, civil engineering, housing, landscaping, librarian, nursing, restaurateur, sculpture and ceramic art, social work, jobs located underground, accounting, and warehousing and storage.

• The **Metal** Person: We might not yet recognize a strongly metal type, but chances are that this person knows us. Analytical, detached, cool, and keenly aware of how things work, including people, the metal person above all has standards and applies them continually. Like autumn, the metal time of year, this individual knows that parsing, pruning, and eliminating are necessary before the next cycle, wherever that may be, can begin.

Metal people are physically shapely, sometimes delicate, sometimes curvaceous; they are often fine-featured, with good skin and hair, and graceful. Metal people are often emotionally reserved, even "dry"; nevertheless they have a sense of beauty and show some kind of pursuit of perfection, often manifesting a strong sense of justice—a passionate devotion to establishing right versus wrong. Mentally, metal people are highly principled, concerned with what's correct and true; they're good at solidifying intuition into clearly defined ideas. Where fire seeks inspiration, metal establishes order. Where wood grows, or grows into, new structures, metal creates form through reduction. Deficiency in metal is seen in shyness, sparse or clumsy speech, obsessive behavior, and being overly independent, even antisocial. Excess metal leads to self-righteousness, tilting at windmills, prying, snooping, and gossip, a fussbudget personality, and one who gives grief over every little perceived violation of decorum. Metal people prefer a dry climate and pungent or savory foods; metal-affiliated parts of the body are the lungs and large intestine. Metal also rules the skin; note the connection, which includes the function of elimination, to the lung and large intestine and to metal's emphasis on boundaries.

Metal professions and activities: banking and finance, beauty products and cosmetic medicine, criticism, electrical engineering, jewelry, railroading, refining, tool and die making, weapons manufacture (waging war and leading troops are more affiliated with wood and fire), and defense contracting.

• The **Water** Person: Do you know someone who seems to have a lot going on beneath the surface? Do you know someone who never stays in one place even when doing nothing? Do you know someone who fits in with any external circumstances? These are all water types. And what do they have in common? Water wants to merge, dissolve, contain or be contained, and connect to other, often deeper, levels of life.

The water physique, typical of water's diversity and "hard to catch" quality, manifests in at least two types: the bony, angular, spry, fast-moving "river" type, and the slow, heavy "ocean" type. For both types, their movements are small, irregular, and easy, whether rapid or ponderous. The water person's thoughts and feelings—usually intertwined—ebb and flow, whether hidden or lying on the surface, whether dense and complex or light and frothy. His or her ideas often move between generalities, even deep wisdom, and momentary minutiae. Because of their relative closeness to dissolution, water people prize self-knowledge yet remain mysterious and are attracted to mystery. They won't hoard, like earth (unless frozen into ice, which isn't nice for them), because they're more interested in moving and connecting. Like human sprinkling cans, water people are good at dispersing ideas, not to mention raining down feelings. Deficiency in water shows as poor judgment, sloth, perversity, hypocrisy, unreliability, flightiness, and maliciousness. Excess water appears as nebulousness, impenetrability, hysteria, and a Byzantine complexity of thought and feeling. Water people prefer a cool climate and like salty foods; water-affiliated parts of the body are the kidneys and bladder.

Water professions and activities: advertising, media and communications, film, glassmaking, music performance, oil and gas industries, postal and Internet systems, utilities, and irregular, arcane, and "odd" jobs. Water people are often drawn to what's strange, neglected, or apparently insignificant; in evolved cases, they intuitively understand the need to give through receiving. As Lao Tsu writes, "The highest form of good is like water: the goodness of water benefits

all things without struggling, even flowing in places that men despise. This is why water is like Tao" (*Tao Te Ching*, Verse 8).

Balancing Our Elements

Traditional Chinese medicine, knowing that all Five Elements have important roles in our lives—physical, emotional, and mental—strives for a harmonic balance that promotes optimal vital energy. This goal is identical in the external environment, hence the development of the practice of feng shui. External imbalances cause problems, as we shall see, just as internal imbalances do, which can lead to poor health and disease. Furthermore, the inner and outer worlds are continuously interacting, with their own balances to maintain. Let's look at Sarah (not her real name), a strongly wood person who worked at a bank, a typical metal-influenced environment, as an administrator. Most wood people enjoy executive tasks, and Sarah did, initially. After this early period of enthusiasm, she got frustrated because that old glass ceiling blocked her wood-inspired desire for expansion and growth. She wanted to quit, but the company felt that she was too valuable an employee; a colleague suggested that she switch into personnel, and she wisely gave it a try—a nice lesson in the rewards of being open to environmental cues! While the destructive cycle comes into play between her company and her personality (metal cuts wood), her new job, moving people about and affiliated with water, supports her type, evoking the metal-water-wood phases of the creative cycle. Thus Sarah is happy at work again, and her performance has been excellent—a fine example of finding success through Five Element dynamics. Another lesson here is to pay attention to what our feelings tell us about imbalances. Sarah's intuition at some point said "Try this," and a new world opened up. As Lao Tsu wrote, "Knowing others is perceptive, but knowing one's own self is enlightened; conquering others shows strength, but conquering one's self shows true power" (*Tao Te Ching,* Verse 33).

Walking the Walk

Really learning the Five Elements means seeing the world in a new way—and also seeing old things in the light of new connections. Let's start with our day: What activities, thoughts, or feelings were connected to water, wood, fire, and so on? For example, sending e-mails to friends often serves a water function; signing up for a class or planning a trip usually connects to wood; and putting things away relates to earth. Reading an article about conservation and checking on a friend's well-being also connect to the earth element. Because this exercise can be literally limitless (here comes a metal function—discrimination!), limit it to fifteen minutes or one notebook page.

Next, on another occasion, let's look at some of the things you feel strongly about (love and hate or fear and grief, and so on) and sense their elemental connection. For example, John Keats's famous ode "To Autumn" is a gorgeous tapestry of earth and metal connections. Read it. Another classic is Gerard Manley Hopkins's "God's Grandeur," with its wood, fire, and water connections. Read that. What do our likes and dislikes in entertainment, art, and leisure say about us? And how about situations at work? What makes us catch fire, so to speak? One colleague loathes becoming overly scheduled, as his water nature strongly dislikes confinement. Again, this exercise can last all day, so set a reasonable limit.

Here's one more: Find a person who strongly connects to each of the Five Elements and write down that person's attributes. Few of us are exclusively or even strongly one type, so we might need to think a bit. Yet sooner or later we'll recall that thoughtful perfectionist (metal) from school or an uncle who collected everything (earth). Consider physical life—body form, movement, posture, health—and how thoughts and feelings all combine to evoke a certain element. As I said before, this exercise should not be shared with the subject.

The Five Elements Outside

We can find the elemental "type" of places and things as we can with people; some locations and objects may show their elemental affiliation in a very obvious way or blend any combination of elements, challenging our sensitivity to find a dominant quality, if it exists. (Perfectly balanced spaces, as with people, do occur, although very rarely.) So this list gives strongly one-type examples so that, with sufficient practice, mixtures of elements can be detected. Remember, too, that we must trust our intuition when it picks up nonobvious connections; truth is, a great deal of environmental energy is hidden.

Wood environments are dominated by tall and thin shapes, such as buttes, volcanic towers, and, of course, trees in the natural world; and man-made structures such as skyscrapers, towers, smokestacks, and minarets. Many modern city centers, with their bunched, slender office towers reaching toward the sky, indeed resemble a forest. In many instances this has created an imbalance in the city, leading to social, emotional, and communication challenges for the residents because too much wood damages earth (which preserves, among other things, family and social relations) and depletes water (which rules communication); on the other hand, these cities abound in creativity, commerce, and money because excess wood stimulates the fire and metal elements. An excellent adjustment is the placement, in between the city's towers, of broad, level parks with ponds and lakes, achieving a balance with stronger earth and water. The plaza in New York City's Lincoln Center, with its broad terraces, fountains, and reflecting pool, is a famous and successful example. Buildings with many tall pillars or columns also evoke wood, as do homes built in the popular English Tudor style. Indeed, any neighborhood that makes us feel like we're walking in a mature forest among tall, healthy trees fills us with wood ch'i.

Considering our intuitive impressions, wood environments feel pioneering, fresh, and full of new growth.

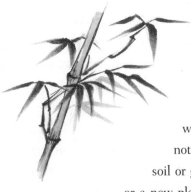

If we get such an impression, say, in the middle of a prairie, it would seem odd, right? But how do we know if there's not a change in the soil or geology beneath us, or a new plant growth about to spring up, or a new owner about to build there? Trust the feeling and study, research, and investigate it!

Fire environments are characterized by sharp, pointed forms, seen in mountains like Wyoming's Grand Tetons; buildings with spires and steeples; and homes with high, pointed gables and roofs. In addition, places where heat is created or chemical transformations take place, such as volcanic areas, refineries, and many factories, belong in the fire category. Fire locations feel dynamic and inspiring (there's a pun: in-*spire*-ing). Fire-type buildings aren't common in many of our newer suburbs, which relates to why so many of them feel sleepy and inactive. In older towns it takes just one high steeple on the village square to create a symboli-cally charged focal point for the whole locale, drawing the eye above the mundane and hinting at transforma-tion or even inspiration. Thus many schools and well-designed office and commercial parks have one high point, such as a bell tower, cupola, or belvedere, to sug-gest a connection with something transformative.

Famous fire structures include the Giza pyramids and European Gothic cathedrals, like those at Char-tres, Salisbury, and Rheims. Note how these important buildings, set on broad open plains, enriched the societ-ies around them on many levels and scales, just as fire and earth are in the creative cycle. A sharp (yes, another pun) reader may ask, what if a fire-element cathedral sits next to a river, as with Notre Dame in Paris? Aren't fire and water in the destructive or restraining cycle? Interestingly, the principal architect of Notre Dame, one Abbot Suger, made the front towers flat, creating a wood shape and introducing the wood element. In this way, the creative cycle is evoked through the sequence of water-wood-fire, and the building has all the more potent vital energy. No one supposes that Abbot Suger studied traditional feng shui; rather, good design utilizes universal principles or archetypes that are intuitively available to everyone. Knowledge of the Five Elements allows us to appreciate and reuse these insights in a clear, creative manner.

Earth environments are marked by flat areas and broad or flat-topped structures, including plateaulike or plainslike spaces and buildings that are, similarly, far wider than they are tall: pueblos, malls, minimalist or so-called modern homes, many types of schools and offices, and warehouses. Most of us would recognize the classic ranch-style home found in countless suburbs. Earth areas feel calm, restrained, and often restful. A major earth function is to preserve and store, and some of these buildings store lots of space. It may seem odd that many school buildings look like warehouses or malls, but learning and inspiration are closely tied to the fire element, and earth follows fire in the creative cycle. In principle, these schools are enriched by thought-provoking and inspirational—fire element—work going on inside. Without effective teachers, of course, schools become just warehouses, keeping kids off the streets. We may notice that many buildings utilize earth-affiliated materials like brick, stucco, and adobe; doesn't that automatically make them earth types? Not necessarily. Yes, some earth-element structures may emphasize brick and adobe as part of a larger design based on low, broad lines. For example, since much of mid-America is broad and flat, it has inspired many similar, earth-affiliated styles; Frank Lloyd Wright's buildings are often strongly earth structures, such as the Kaufmann House (Fallingwater) in Pennsylvania and Chicago's Robie House. On the other hand, the brick and stone Smith-sonian Institution in Washington, D.C., strongly evokes fire and wood. We need to feel how shape and function, style and setting, all blend together, the way many notes can form a distinctive melody. As the old saying goes, architecture is the music of space, and there may be multiple themes.

Metal environments are revealed by an abundance of rounded forms: round hills or mountains—parts of the Appalachians are fine examples; rolling landscapes, and buildings with domes or round sides. Metal locations create a feeling of harmony, balance, and orderliness—while landscapes with too much metal can feel fussy or overly planned. Recall the metal person's love of perfection: The circle has been known throughout history as the perfect form. Interestingly, the Earth's spherical core is mostly metal—molten iron and nickel. It's frequently remarked that banks and financial institutions often have domes, because money is affiliated with the metal element. Well-known examples stretch from coast to coast: New York's World Financial Center and Williamsburg Bank, Philly's Girard Trust, Ohio's Cleveland Trust, Denver's Wells Fargo tower, and San Francisco's Hibernia and Humboldt banks. But as with all generalities, we must be careful; the U.S. Capitol has a great dome, and the U.S. government is greatly in debt at the moment. Good energy arises more from the flow between elements than from emphasizing any one element. Moreover, when metal is at its best, the hoarding impulse found in strong earth gives way to principled, careful use. In financial terms, prudent investment of funds is almost always better than socking money away.

Metal buildings are also characterized by the use of metal in their construction, such as the shiny aluminum skin seen on many skyscrapers. A related question arises: Does using such materials trump shape in determining a building's elemental affiliation? For example, if an aluminum skyscraper has a wood shape, what's its type? That depends on which attribute is stronger, and, in any case, a mixture is a mixture, like the Notre Dame Cathedral mentioned above. It's more important, in the case of this skyscraper, to see how the metal and wood, symbolizing restraint versus growth, and generalization versus discrimination, which are in the destructive cycle, play off each other. If the energy is off, and if there are tensions and troubles in such a wood-metal environment, what should we do? One creative possibility is to consider what effect elemental water would have on the situation.

Water environments are dominated by sinuous, undulating shapes and wavy, gently curving forms as well as anything irregular, haphazard, and turbulently complex. South Dakota's Badlands and Cape Cod's dune country are strong natural examples; striking man-made examples include the Sydney Opera House, which is shaped like waves heading toward a beach; Antoni Gaudí's Casa Milà in Barcelona, which looks like it melted under a heat lamp; and many university campuses, which swirl together willy-nilly, as in a gumbo, sections of modern, Gothic, and classical architecture. These environments can feel mysterious, sublime, scary, cold, wild, or even comical—quite a grab bag! Water environments can be, naturally, dominated by the physical presence of water, such as riverbanks, lakesides, marshes, and estuaries.

Clear glass (which is chemically not a true solid, meaning noncrystalline) is affiliated with the water element and an important modern building material. Glass thus mixes well with wood and metal; many of us can remember the original McDonald's franchise hamburger stand, with its two large yellow arches (metal) flanking a simple shed with lots of glass. This design synched up with the company's greatest success (and much credit is certainly due to founder Ray Kroc, Jr.). Note that the franchise's current flat, boxy, brown-brick design, which emphasizes earth, evokes a much larger, entrenched, perhaps slower, company. Returning to our discussion of materials, mixing glass with earth or fire elements can create a harsh dynamic, as it evokes the destructive cycle. Boston's City Hall is a brooding example of "neo-brutalist" architecture, with many irregular glass windows set in an overhanging concrete mesa. Whether its energy has something to do with Boston's public-sector problems is a deeper question, but in its plaza with a large circular or spherical sculpture, replacing a defunct fountain would be a good thing. Composite materials are also becoming common, and plastic, for one, is part of the water element. Water may seem like a catch-all element, and, in many ways, it is the strangest, most mysterious, and most slippery of the five. Nevertheless, visionary architects seem to be turning more and more to water-inspired forms in order to create something special with public structures and spaces.

Many of the most satisfying and inspiring edifices in the world combine all five elements smoothly and achieve a powerful harmony. One famous case study is the Taj Mahal. It has a striking, rounded dome and a brilliantly white exterior (metal) set symmetrically among four prominent minarets (wood). The dome and the many arches throughout the structure end in sharp points (fire); there are also many small spires on the roof. Reflecting pools, canals, and watercourses shimmer around the main building, and much of the detailed ornamentation in the walls is irregular and wavy (water). The whole structure sits on a broad, flat base, surrounded by low, level gardens (earth). Everything is balanced and in proportion. Its ch'i flows easily and moderately. Take any one of these elements away and the magic isn't quite right. A whole book could be written about the energetic harmony of this amazing building. In general, when each of the elements has a harmonious role in some structure or organization, the chances for success through creative development are multiplied, as are the ways to resist damage or decay.

The Five Elements Indoors

As we've seen in exterior environments, the elements express themselves in many ways—as many ways as energy and matter/materials can manifest—and the same is true for the inside. To keep things simple, we begin looking at the indoor elements in pure, direct, and approachable forms, with short lists that generalize common Five Element associations. An easy and common example is that glassware relates to the water element. However, we must remember that when we actually practice, we take into account *all* the details of each item's shape, substance, use, feeling, and so on, and then sense how these details connect to one element or another, maybe all five or just one. Perfectly round, silvery glassware can evoke metal more than water, for example. In another instance, bookcases store books, a function typically connected to earth. However, the bookcase might be tall and narrow and built of wood, which all relate to the wood element. Or the bookcase may have glass shelving, metal supports, pointed finials, and so on. But we need to begin with the following obvious generalizations in order to transcend them:

Wood: pillars, columns, easels, floor lamps, houseplants, most chairs, pianos, stereo speakers, tall, thin furniture such as hutches, cabinets, and highboys, many bookcases, artists' materials, writing desks, and artists' work areas.

Fire: fireplaces and furnaces, firearms and guns, leather and animal products, ovens and stoves, uncaged pets, some computers and their functions, study areas, pointed or sharply angled furniture, intense kinds of art, and objects with spikes and points. Hats and masks relate to the head, which is affiliated with fire.

Earth: carpets, cushions, most beds, dressers, closets and storage areas, pottery, ceramics and stoneware, broad or low tables, computers if their functions are primarily data storage, shelving, garages, basements, and tunnels.

Metal: globes, most appliances, money, pipes, round (not pointed) arches, display swords and shields, many tools and hardware, round tables and round objects, such as portraits and mirrors, and metal furniture in general.

Water: clear glass and glassware, most televisions, sinks, laundries, baths, fountains, showers, sheer or flowing curtains, petroleum products such as plastics (remember that their shape, such as a sphere or spire, may bring in the influence of another element), synthetics, and irregularly shaped furniture.

More about mirrors: Although they are a type of glass and thus materially affiliated with water, the elemental connection of mirrors is more influenced by their shape and the area they're placed in. Because mirrors catch our eyes reflexively and have a strong influence on a room's light and how space is perceived, mirrors should be used mindfully. Many beginning feng shui practitioners overuse them, like overly solicitous doctors who prescribe painkillers for every discomfort.

Walking the Walk

We need to recognize the Five Elements at work in our environment, so spend a moment in at least a few important spaces, such as the office, living room, bedroom, kitchen, garden, and so on, and study the elemental affiliations of that space and of the objects in it. Write down all colors, textures, shapes, and compositions. Inventory how things feel: Do some areas give a strong vibe of growth or transformation? Of preservation or discrimination or merging/dissolution? Some objects that might at first feel one way may change later, which is fine; just follow your intuition. For example, a painting in one person's office at first looked broad and flat, so the owner reasoned that it had an earth shape. Then she felt that because it was a picture of horses crossing a stream and their shapes were irregular and complex, it was more connected to water. But she finally concluded that the horses' sharp ears, tails, and manes and their strong movement felt fiery, which became a conscious discovery of the painting's ultimately inspiring quality: That's fire! This process is the right way to go, for our *impressions* are what matter here. The more we can sense our own impressions the more successful will be our efforts to find harmony in our environment.

On another occasion, choose a favorite building to study, whether it be the Parthenon, Hearst Castle, or Grandma's house, and figure out the elemental connections as we did with the Taj Mahal. Be creative; one student visited a steel mill, another a dairy barn. It's almost always better to visit this site in person, but if you know it very well, you can use your imagination—as long as you can imagine it in sufficient detail. You should be able to recall, for example, what every side of the building looks like. The same goes for every interior space. Write about any shapes, materials, colors, contents, and above all, feelings, you encounter. What makes this place attractive or interesting? What's unappealing about it, if anything?

CHAPTER FOUR

The Vital Energy of the Home and Business Environments

The goodness of the house is in its place on Earth; the
goodness of the heart, in its deep serenity.

—Tao Te Ching, Verse 8

s Lao Tsu shows in the words quoted above, a good space and a good frame of mind are closely linked. So we begin our discussion of how to visit a site by looking first inward, then outward. In both cases, as we learn about the spaces in which we spend our lives, we begin with the bigger picture and work down to the smaller details.

Preparations for Visiting a Site

Whether we're checking out a place for the first time or looking over the old homestead for the seven millionth time, the state we're in has a great deal to do with what we see and what we pay attention to. Our energy affects a site's energy, our ch'i its ch'i. For beginners and experts alike, the personal preparation we make before feng shui work is critical. We are the instruments of perception, so we need to be warmed up and in tune so we can resonate with a multitude of new, sometimes surprising, impressions. Performing a site inspection is very different from going to the library, the doctor's office, or the shopping mall. In doing feng shui, we need to use our bodies, our feelings, and our intellects all together at once, and at a finer level than usual. Bringing body, heart, and brain together—how can we prepare to do that? In Verse 16 of the *Tao Te Ching,* Lao Tsu tells us to "Let yourself become utterly empty and repose in deep tranquility. Then will you observe the various things of the world together take form and then in tranquility return to their source . . . to realize this process brings insight and illumination."

So what we need to do is clear the decks, so to speak, of all mental, physical, and emotional activity and allow our different parts to come together as a whole. Lao Tsu says that this can be done with a complete inner and outer stillness, which many readers may recognize as a primary goal of meditation. Now we could fill at least one room of a house with how-to books on meditation from the last ten years alone. Here we keep it simple and stick to our basic Taoist principles, particularly the Yin/Yang polarity. The key is to become "utterly empty." A popular yet ancient method, for example, is to sit on a cushion and let the body completely relax, let the heart calm down, and let all thoughts drift off as we did in the very first exercise (pages 17–18). You stay aware of yourself as much as possible, but you don't try to *do* anything; emptiness happens—you are aware of how active, bubbling, and chaotic, how Yang, our different parts can be. Then let the natural transformation from Yang to Yin unfold. When you become as Yin as possible, like the deep of night, a new sort of thoughtfulness and presence soon dawns. The point of this new Yang is to bring us into a better whole, into more of a unity. For some practitioners, walking slowly and silently in a garden or lying down in a quiet space works just as well. Whatever method we choose, we become totally receptive to the new, the other, the different—a naturally Taoist way of beginning a Taoist activity—feng shui.

After this preparation through repose, you can inspect a site with heightened senses and a heightened sensitivity. If, during the preparation, your inner state doesn't feel right, or you're still upset because a check just bounced or a spouse yelled at you, don't force the issue. It's better to avoid any attempt at finding the intuitive sensitivity required by feng shui than to risk missing or distorting important impressions from the environment. Since this preparatory empty, receptive state is so important, several works in the bibliography give additional resources for the study of Taoist meditation.

Thus we begin by looking at the site, which is simply the patch of planet Earth where we work or dwell. The biggest financial and emotional decision some of us will ever make is whether to buy a piece of property, with or without buildings on it, for home or business. How can feng shui help us evaluate a site? If we already have a home or business, how can we improve that site by nurturing environmental harmony? If there are problems with it, what can be done to improve the situation? What adjustments can be made to the site to improve its value or increase the success of its activities? We have already touched upon the tools to answer these questions and have used them in the exercises. Now we put them all—deep intuition, the play of opposites, vital energy, and creative/destructive elements, also described as aspects of Tao, Yin/Yang, ch'i, and the Five Elements—to work in a more direct way.

Influences on a Site's Ch'i

In a state of attentive, alert repose, in which you're open to new impressions, try to sense the full spectrum of a location's energy. What we've learned earlier about ch'i will still apply—attending to balance, flow, and authenticity—now in specific situations. Begin by looking at the people-scape—how previous occupants, both recent and distant, still influence the site—as well as the landscape and its visible *and* invisible influences.

1. **Historic Predecessor Energies**. Does it matter who inhabited our space in the past, whether fifteen or five hundred years ago? Yes! All energy is a vibration of

some kind, and although vibrations dis-
sipate, they don't die. The further back
in time we look, however, smaller events
lose their potency in the face of the larger,
more intense, and more widespread occur-
rences. Native peoples lived in almost all
parts of the United States for thousands
of years. In most cases they were killed,
starved, sickened, or forcibly removed from
their homes, and in many ways this "trail
of tears" still has not ended. How can we
improve such "heavy" negative ch'i? Consciousness becomes paramount. One possible response would be to first, within
each one of our own spiritual traditions,
meditate, pray, or make some plea for help
from a greater power to heal old wounds.
Properly used and authentic Native rituals (some of which are described later) still
have their power as well. Then consider
supporting indigenous arts and crafts by
placing an appealing artifact, barring any
elemental affinity problems, in the home
or office. Just tuning to the present reality

of Native Americans affects our ch'i; supporting their educational, scholarship, or health programs is often a natural outcome. Another example of bad historical ch'i involves the slave trade, from which many eastern seaports profited before 1809. For example, a musician with exceptional sensitivity moved to Providence, Rhode Island, which was once the largest slave trafficking port in New England, and was quickly surprised and a bit frightened at the presence of angry ghosts that she felt were still roaming there. What could she do to help *that* ch'i? Again, our various spiritual traditions all have methods: Native Americans regularly burn sage leaves, and southern Chinese burn dried orange peel. On a different level, the musician became more attuned to the racism still flourishing in the world and from just about all groups. On rare occasions, a historic event unfolds in our own backyard, such as the destruction of New York's World Trade Center, and intense negative energy must be dealt with promptly. At a gathering of park employees in downtown Manhattan, for example, several traumatized workers held a simple Plains Indian healing ritual not long after the attack. A medicine chief prayed and brushed an eagle feather fan over the mute horticulturalists and gardeners, cleansing them symbolically of spiritual debris and death ch'i; the ceremony allowed many to grieve as a group and release blocked feelings. So, in sum, there are many levels on which ghosts need to leave. If your efforts feel incomplete after sincere effort, you can consult an expert.

2. **Immediate Predecessor and Neighbor Energies**. The more recent our predecessors the more likely that any small (though not to those involved) upheavals and local cataclysms will still hang in the air. Who lived in or worked in the site before us? You need to do a little homework and find out their story. If the place is a business and the predecessor went bankrupt, you certainly don't want to

absorb any of the vibes left over from that! Cleanse and purify the property, removing all traces of the failed enterprise that can be removed. And what can't be removed should be altered—subtly is fine—with your own marks or designs, such as a coat of paint, different lighting, and a new lay-out for starters. Additional examples are listed below. And the work doesn't end here, either; you must remain continu-ally sensitive to the possible actions of old, bad ch'i. If the predecessors in your house divorced and moved away, do you feel any strains in your relationships? If the former occupants had problems with their chil-dren, is there an echo of those problems beginning to appear? One way to both counteract bad energy and remember to pay attention to warning signs is to place on the site an unobtrusive object thought-fully chosen to reflect the concern. If the previous occupants had a bad split, con-sider one of the many small and beauti-ful symbols of fidelity and loyalty, such as dogs, wheat ears, rings, rosemary, garnet stones, and doves or other creatures that mate for life. If the predecessors had financial trouble, find an appealing prosperity symbol; depending on your tradition, this could be a fish, an elephant, deer tracks, jade plants, or turquoise stones. Don't, however, just order the first thing you see in a catalog without doing some homework, don't get the brightest or shiniest thing you can find, and don't put the piece in a pachysandra in a casual or offhand way; inner sincerity, focus, and concentration are required for success. Great size, expense, or flashiness in the offering can actually work at cross-purposes to your desired end. Tao usually favors the small, the subtle, the humble, and the rarely noticed. In the Taoist martial art of t'ai ch'i, there is a saying that four ounces of force can deflect ten tons of opposition. How is this possible? By letting the overly strong overextend itself and turn into its opposite, Yang into Yin.

In many cases the immediate predecessor left the site harmoniously or without misfortune; nevertheless, respect their ch'i, for it can be powerful. This point is strongly made by the case of a farmer in the Midwest who planted an English walnut tree near his home. He lavished great care and attention on it, as if it were a beloved pet or even a child. When the farmer died, the new owner of the home thought the walnut tree a nuisance in the efficient cutting of the lawn, and he chopped it down. The new owner soon became sickly and spent his remaining few years in and out of the hospital. This is also a lesson in respecting natural features of the site that may shelter spirits or esoteric forces. How many of us self-styled modern, advanced humans have lost our natural ability to feel higher and subtler energies? Most of us! So never cut down a plant, move a rock, dig a hole, or disrupt the natural world without first meditating on the action and *asking permission* of the resident spirits to go ahead with the "surgery." If it's a bad idea, we'll feel it, like butterflies in the stomach or gooseflesh on the back of the neck. Moreover, to ask permission to change the site reminds us to remain humble, mindful of our brief walk on Earth and of our smallness in the face of nature's greatness.

While we're on the topic of human energies, let's talk about dealing with neighbors. There's no question that the people living or working around us will have an influence on the energy of our site—as we will on *their* energy. This is another thoroughly good reason to follow the Golden Rule. Nevertheless, it may happen that, much beyond our control, bad ch'i is coming from next door. It could be loud music late on weeknights, uncovered garbage next to the property line, a barking dog, or, for one family, the hot exhaust from a neighbor's outdoor HVAC condenser. These intimately human challenges are among the trickiest in life, and a great chance to put Tao to work for us. Without any preconceptions, baggage, or "self" involved, can we understand the opposing energies involved in the problem? Is there a positive change that can naturally evolve out of the situation? What does our intuition tell us? We usually find that there's much we don't know. Begin by just making a connection in a positive, objective spirit; surprising results often follow. Let our "checklist" for preparing to confer (not confront) with the neighbor be Verse 8 from the *Tao Te Ching*:

> The goodness of the heart is in its deep serenity; the goodness of society is in its

humanity; of speaking, in its truthfulness; of
leadership, in its justice; of work, in its skill;
and of action, proper timing.

In the case of the loud music on weeknights, the
offended party had assumed that any "noise" after nine
p.m. was wrong, whereas the partiers, more urban types,
felt than anything before eleven was cool. Somebody
suggested a ten p.m. compromise, and everyone man-
aged to live with it. The homeowner with the outdoor
HVAC unit, with an awakened sense of responsibility,
installed an exhaust baffle on the unit when his neighbor offered to help set it up and even share costs. Amica-
bility reigned. Such suppleness is not always possible; in
the case of the barking dog, repeated entreaties finally
revealed that the owner's daughter, who had thought
that a puppy was her heart's true desire, had no actual
interest in caring for a real pet. After the ASPCA was
called, the dog was sent to the country and, we hope, a
happier life. On the other hand, the uncovered garbage
turned out to be a manifestation of that homeowner's
latent resentment of his neighbor's ethnicity, a not too
subtle message saying "I think you're trash." How much
evil in the world has such small, petty beginnings? In

such cases we revert to laws: The city health department was brought in and issued a fine before the garbage got cleaned up. After that, the old New England farmer's saying held true: "Good fences make good neighbors."

3. **Visible Powers of the Landscape**. It's a shame that many Americans believe they must leave the country to see exotic and striking natural beauty; what's right here in the United States is stunning, although much is threatened with environmental degradation. And if not always postcard quality, the national geography is richly diverse. If your site lies on the Great Plains between the Dakotas and

Minnesota down to Texas, chances are the terrain is flat or gently rolling, especially near rivers. Farther west or near the Appalachians, the ground can be hilly or mountainous. Coastal areas show the influence of the oceans or the Great Lakes, and there may be marshes, inlets, and bays. Much of the Southwest is arid or fully desert, while the Southeast, especially Florida, is subtropical and tropical—wet and hot. The northernmost states often have coniferous forests and seven months of snow. Intelligent, sensitive architecture will literally build upon local conditions, materials, and features. It's a good thing that more and more architects and designers are tuning in to local ecologies and seeing their spaces as part of a continuous natural fabric. So should we all.[1] Isn't it a little crazy to see a veranda-draped plantation-style home that would work perfectly with the natural conditions in Charleston plunked down near Minneapolis, or a heavily bricked Tudor with small, mullioned windows and acres of steep, black roof (to drop all that snow) thrown up in an Miami suburb? Not that every midwestern building should have a cookie-cutter Frank Lloyd Wright Prairie style design, or every southwestern structure a flat massing of white adobe. Yet there really is something called the "genius loci," or the spirit of the place, that we need to work with on some level to develop the best possible environmental energy. Wright's buildings capture—embrace and re-create—something essential about their locale, in the way that many indigenous structures, like the Taos Pueblo, do. Traditional people treat these genius loci as literal spirits and involve them in many aspects of their lives. It's amazing how the "genius loci" will often manifest itself in animal form; Japan's rare Iriomote cat looks like she jumped right out of a Hokusai print, but she was "Japanese" thousands of years before there was a Japan! The same goes for China's snub-nosed monkey, who would look Chinese in the middle of, say, a Brazilian zoo. Plants, too, often capture some of the essence of a place, from French chestnuts to Australian eucalyptus; it's no wonder our ancestors used them in sacred ceremonies linking Earth to Heaven.

Today it's still wise to honor the character of our out-of-doors environment inside our home and office. For example, a New England family puts purple and white pieces of sea-polished abalone shell, the prized "wampum" of the Wampanoag Tribe, in a bowl on their dining room table. A financier in Tucson highlights her living room with striking slabs of petrified wood. A family in Michigan uses glacier-carved lake stones as bookends, paperweights, and doorstops. These placements feel right because a home or office is not just a place for ourselves but a place in which we and our world must interact. Psychologists and researchers have found that people who feel connected to their local landscape tend to be more relaxed, comfortable, and perceptive in their daily living, including their business affairs. In feng shui terms, such people have stronger natural flow and authenticity in their ch'i.

Given all this variety in our local landscape, what else we can do to harmonize our site with the local ch'i? Start with what you can see: sight lines, which are easily described as prominent, recurring views and have some kind of psychological effect on the viewer. Often we'll have no control over scenes that are less than pleasing; the office window may overlook a freight yard, or the bedroom window may line up with a neighbor's obnoxiously pink-painted garage. Sometimes we can block such sight lines by placing things with good energy on our own property. In the example of the neighbor's ugly garage, planting tall marsh or prairie grasses or a bamboo stand in front would cover up the visual offense with something attractive and right for the landscape. But sometimes you can't block a bad sight line, so then you can distract or overpower the negative view with something positive. For example, put some beautiful or meaningful framed photos on the windowsill or compelling pictures next to the (usually drawn) blinds. They'll take your emotional eye, so to speak, to a much better place every time your eyes stray toward that ugly freight yard. With the opposite situation, when there is a rewarding sight line, play it up: arrange chairs or desks so so you can get the best views possible. This can be more rewarding than the "commanding position" for your desk, which has become a feng shui cliché. Indeed, there shouldn't be clichés because everyone's situation is different. An executive who's attuned to environmental influences turned the back of his chair to the door (gasp!) so he could look out his window at the New York harbor and the Statue of Liberty. And business is prospering.

A more extreme example is the family who fell in love with a wonderful home for sale, perfect in every way, except that it was within view of a cemetery. Traditional feng shui would say to take a pass on the property or else erect elaborate "cures," as they're called, on the sight line, like large statues of dragons. Well, there are cases of the "cure" statuary making the other residents more irritated by the funky statues than by the local grave sites. Moreover, sometimes it's better to, forgive the pun, think outside the box. For the spiritually evolved buyer, such a location offers the opportunity for frequent meditation of the most powerful kind on the ultimate given in life, one that is honored at the highest levels of Buddhism, Christianity, and Judaism, among other paths. And such a property might be a heck of a deal. So the question is really about where we are in terms of our spiritual needs and abilities.

- If your site is on a slope, hillside, or incline, be aware, and in extreme cases *beware,* of the ch'i flowing down on and around your building. We often see that this side of a house is quietest in terms of human activity because it's the most turbulent area of wind, rain, runoff, and other natural forces; our bodies instinctively avoid it like fish avoid eddies. If the downward rush of energy is too strong, one possible adjustment is to place a strong outdoor or garden element to break the flow like the bow of a boat would do. If the climate permits, you could use large rhododendrons clumped around a stone lantern, bench, or statue. There are fine types of shrubbery for every climate, and even ornamental cacti for desert environments.

For similar reasons, avoid all energy flows that point right at your building, such as roads, streams or ditches, paths, and power lines. Again, we want to stop the ch'i from hitting the building directly. A straight sidewalk or street aimed at your home or office can be blocked or baffled with appropriate landscaping; yet in some cases bushes and trees aren't enough to block strong energy flows, and more aggressive adjustments must be found. To defang the threatening appearance of a power line on the property, for example, the fix should feel forceful. Some effective choices are a stone or picket fence, an arbor, a decorative gate, a garden pool, or an antique hand p u m p — a n d note the fire and water elements used here  to control too much metal (we'll thoroughly explore elemental adjustments in the next chapter). The best idea is to use things that curve and meander to slow down any overly aggressive vital energy, making it gentle and tractable. In Hong Kong, a city where even the bus drivers profess to be feng shui aficionados, the Disney Company spent a fortune at its park to make the main entrance road undulate instead of lie straight. And this is naturally, organically wise—see page 245 to understand the problems that direct energy flows can bring, in the case of New Orleans.

In the same way, other buildings or large objects—outcroppings, walls, fences—can make us feel psychologically threatened if they "point" or show a corner toward our building. These corners are traditionally called "secret arrows" because symbolically they look like they will stab our site. To blunt the point of these "arrows," vigorous plantings, trellises, statuary, fountains, and even toolsheds and screens are effective. Similarly, sites near busy roads, highways, and rail lines get a lot of turbulent ch'i even if the sources don't point right at them. Major adjustments are the rule here, including dense plantings, often in combination with large walls. Architecturally speaking, the South Asian scheme of an inward-turned building, with a serene central court and heavy, fortresslike outer walls, works well in areas of loud, clashing environmental energy.

- If the site is on the top of a rise or hill, or similarly in the middle of a large, flat plain, there is a danger of exposure to too much atmospheric ch'i. Without enough trees, bushes, outbuildings, and other landscape elements around the building, the occupants will become agitated, restless, inflexible, and "dried out." This effect is strongly corroborated by people exposed to such famously adverse, dry winds such as Southern California's Santa Ana, France's *mistral,* and the German *Föhn.* Placing a fountain on the most exposed side can be very helpful, as is some sort of tree planting; tough, strong trees, such as oaks, walnuts, hickories, and some conifers can stand up to big winds. In many parts of the country, these winds come from the northwest, so always check that corner of the property. On the subject of trees and wind, never let a tree touch the building or grow within five feet or so of the walls. Besides the practical need to avoid damage from heaving branches, traditional feng shui practitioners have observed that "touching trees" can serve as conduits for unwanted energies—as the Chinese put it, dragons sometimes live in trees. Are these energies always negative? No, but we need to know our trees, which should be like knowing old friends with whom we share space: Some need to be reined in, others left alone, and others nurtured. In general, living too close together irritates both parties. In addition, many folks think that trees are just some occasional nuisance living on their property, when it's more true that we're guests living on *their* property—if you haven't felt the ch'i of a 350-year-old oak, try sitting with it for a while. And the benefits of trees are legion; the savings in electricity from reduced air-conditioning alone are significant.

In these over-air-conditioned times, note the wind patterns on your site, which may change with the seasons, and try to capture as much fresh air as possible. In the summer, for example, night breezes can cool the home if the windows on opposing sides are open between eleven p.m. and seven a.m. The famous New Orleans "shotgun" house, which spread all over the South, evolved from this idea: The house would face a river or lake, with a porch to shade the front windows, and there were no hallways. Thus air had to flow through the living room, bedroom, and kitchen, front to back; in combination with high ceilings, the house was cooled naturally. Moreover, the original versions were built with local old cypress, which naturally resists high heat and humidity, and even limited flooding.[2]

- If the site is near the bottom of a hollow or valley, a danger often arises from trapped and stagnant ch'i—wind, water, and so forth enter but cannot easily exit. The remedy is suggested by the behavior of water itself, which just keeps flowing on by necessity; it fills a space to form a lake or pond until it finds an outlet. So with this kind of site, create an exit stream leading away from the building either with real water or, symbolically, with plantings, pebbled pathways, walks, or lighting. These streams are almost always gently curved, so that the ch'i can leave in a relaxed, unhurried way— always find that balance between too much and too little. Related to this, beware of bridges, which are another source of stagnant ch'i. The many fairy tales and fables about trolls and ogres living under bridges are not coincidental; pockets of stagnant energy frequently form there, often with dark shadows and bad smells. If your own site is nearby, you can introduce cleansing energies in that direction through lively and colorful landscaping, bright plants, outdoor lights, and symbolic art.

Some of us may have heard that traditional feng shui considers the most optimum siting of a building to be the "armchair" formation, where the structure is backed by a gentle slope that levels off before the rear of the building, and braced on either side by small rises, the larger to the east. These features have charming directional names like tortoise, dragon, tiger, and phoenix. But it's rare to find a site like this, and, moreover, it might be too cozy a site for a dynamic enterprise like a sales hub, where people need to get in and out quickly. Modern feng shui takes the attitude that almost any site can be harmonized, and your house should be optimal for who you are.

4. **Hidden Powers of the Landscape**. There are significant sources of both good and bad energy that cannot be sensed immediately, whether by eye, ear, nose, touch, or feel. With a little training, and sometimes special tools, we can develop our intuition and detect these energies, which are often hidden processes, both large and subtle, of the Earth. As Taoists see the Earth as alive, we need to tune in to her schemes and moods. Just as acupuncturists trace energy flows in the body, so must we study the movement of ch'i in the Earth. Positive energy

often moves along meridians, or ley lines, as the British call them, which underlie a number of significant historical and sacred sites. One in Britain connects Avebury, Stonehenge, and a number of other ancient stone circles; one in France underlies Chartres, which was a religious center as far back as the Neolithic period. Japan's first imperial capital, at Nara, was founded in 710 C.E. after feng shui experts who were brought from T'ang Dynasty China carefully selected a positive confluence of meridians. On the other hand, some movements are dangerous: geologic fault lines, for example, which are cracks in the Earth's shifting surface plates, may threaten entire cities, such as Los Angeles, Tokyo, and San Francisco. Speaking of knowing what's going on beneath our feet, not many folks know that there's a huge, unstable fault in southeastern Missouri (New Madrid); if it slips it could shatter buildings from St. Louis to Memphis. Smaller fractures can be found throughout most states; even granite-bedded New York City had a small quake in 1984. Old, slow (by our time scale) changes in our local geology can also have a strong impact on the energy in the area. Many vivid examples are found in South Dakota's Black Hills, where layers representing more than two billion years of geologic evolution are churned together. Inside this frozen turbulence of rock and earth are found deposits of gold, silver, and uranium, as well as two of the world's five largest cave systems, with many underground rivers and lakes. The fauna and flora above are unique in many ways, and many travelers report strange sensations upon entering; some note that their dogs get very squirrelly. On Bear Butte, one's hair often stands on end from the accumulation of electrostatic charges. Native peoples found intense spiritual forces and connections here.

On most sites, however, we need to amplify and detect the underlying energies. Some of these hidden influences are subtle but not trivial—small amounts of radioactivity in the ground can leak into your building in the form of radon, a colorless, odorless gas that is carcinogenic. Radon shouldn't have a chance to accumulate if you follow the principle of keeping ch'i flowing, which requires you to ventilate the basement and get rid of stagnant air. If you're concerned about radon, most municipalities now test free of charge. Another common possibility is that a small underground stream may run below your site. These streams are called "dragon veins" by the Chinese, who believe that they weaken our health. Indeed, there are many reports of people getting headaches and having concentration problems if their bed or desk sits above or next to some kind of water flow. One hypothetical explanation for this is that the moving water creates a low-level electrical field, but whatever the mechanism, avoid these placements if possible. (If the siting can't be avoided, see the Five Element adjustments for excess water described in the next chapter.) One of the most useful tools for detecting hidden energies is dowsing, which is perfectly appropriate for beginners.

Dowsing—A Short Introduction

Dowsing is an art as well as a science, as old as feng shui and civilization itself, and you can become proficient with a little intensive practice. (There are many resources that can be found on the Internet for specific topics and practices, such as dowsing for water, ley lines, precious substances, and so forth; many will tell you how to get specialized tools for these investigations.)

The simplest dowsing tool is a pendulum, that is, a piece of string or cord with a weight attached to one end. Beyond that, you can get creative: Some dowsers swear by silk strings and quartz crystal weights, so you can experiment with materials that appeal to your sensibility. Once you have a pendulum ready for use, take a few moments to clear your thoughts through a calming meditation and relax as much as possible. When you feel you're ready, stand in what feels like a neutral area, which could be the middle of a quiet, spacious room or the

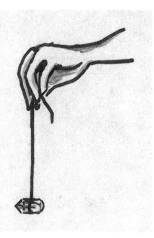

yard. Then hold the pendulum with one or both hands at least a foot in front of you, letting it come completely to rest. Then "tune" your pendulum by asking it an obvious yes-or-no question, like "Is today Wednesday?" For some people a move to the left means yes; for others a little hitch to the right means yes. Beginners may be surprised to find that after a few moments the weight seems to just displace itself, usually a small but distinct move. You may have to run a few trials to get normal consistency, but with practice you can relax, and relaxation brings synchrony. Next, go to as many areas on your site as necessary and simply ask, with your inner voice, "Is there good energy here?" Many are surprised by the results. It's a good idea to dowse with these same questions on another day, in the event that some of the ch'i shifts during the natural cycles of the month. As for monthly cycles, women should not dowse or conduct similar rituals during their "moon" time, as Native Americans respectfully call the menses.

If after repeated attempts the pendulum method of dowsing puts you completely at sixes and sevens, here's a neat alternative that's tailored to detecting ch'i. "Wise women" (often derogatorily called "witches" in patriarchal cultures) in the Celtic tradition have used a technique for centuries that's a variation on a tool called a Schumann rod. Take two identical coat hangers and hold one in each hand as follows: With your palms flat and facing up, partly curl your fingers so they form a groove where they join the hand. Rest the center of the long side of the hanger in this groove so that the hook points down. With both hangers so positioned, press the backs of the middle joints of your fingers on one hand against the backs of the middle joints of the other. Relax the thumbs. The hooks below should now be about one to two inches apart and able to swing easily back and forth. Hold the hangers about a foot in front of you and proceed just as if you were using a pendulum. The hooks may widen their gap in response to positive energy, or they may narrow. You'll need to experiment and find out; it is somewhat uncanny to see them move when the energy changes, and they're highly responsive. So when you find centers of good and bad energy, consider moving the desk, bed, or favorite chair to that spot, and see how it feels. In experimenting, there is no wrong approach. The point is to learn and have fun with dowsing as well—there's no limit to what you can discover.

Walking the Walk

Sometimes the most enlightening way to feel the ch'i of a site is to use atypical, noneveryday powers of observation, stimulating the intuition and relaxing the rational, bookkeeping mind. For example, there's a potent exercise called active imagination: In a secluded spot without distractions, recall all aspects of the location in question from trivial to critical that you can. Then stop and empty your mind—as we've been practicing since Chapter One—for at least a moment as the Yin phase takes hold. Then recall the site and let your imagination run free to play with the pictures in whatever way it likes. Pay attention to any distortions or odd changes. For some this task will be difficult, but with practice it will become more and more effective. Beginners can put on training wheels, so to speak: First, try to imagine the site as an animal. Whatever pops up, accept it; watch the animal, and let it convey something. It may transform from one image to another. For example, one home-owner imagined a big, misshapen rock in her backyard as a gray toad spitting sparks. This made her realize that the rock bothered her on an unconscious level, and she screened it off with a mass of colorful shrubs and flow-ers (removing large stones, especially if they're deeply buried, can be expensive and disruptive).

Another exercise is to see the site as a plant. Don't feel that this plant must have "normal" or con-ventional features. One businessman imagined his office as a J. K. Rowling (Harry Potter) sort of composite pear tree that was overgrown in some spots, hiding valuable stuff, aggressively smacking him with branches in other instances, and even sending vinelike branches to other rooms where stuff was left. Vigorous pruning and training of this creature was very helpful to the owner's business.

CHAPTER FIVE

Enriching Home and Business Sites with the Five Elements

ontinuing our efforts to bring harmony between our home or office and
its environment, we circle back (pun
intended!) to the Five Elements. As
we've learned earlier, these elements
are five phases of change found throughout the natural
world and are symbolized by wood, fire, earth, metal,
and water. In more abstract terms, these symbols are
connected to growth, transformation, preservation, discrimination, and dissolution. They form two cycles in
which each element feeds or is fed by another, and each
element diminishes or is diminished by another. They
appear in a site as forms or shapes, materials, activities,

and overall feel. We then find that most environments, buildings, rooms, and furnishings evoke one of these elements more than another; our goal is to keep this manifestation healthy, neither too strong nor too weak, and in sync with our own lives. When the elements of our site are in balance, they function optimally; from this harmony our various activities and resources are supported, our ability to create is enhanced, and our sharing and enjoyment of life are increased.

Every building is, in a manner of speaking, a frozen moment of design, engineering, technology, construction materials, customs, and chance, assembled to satisfy the needs of a certain person or people at a specific time and place. And almost every one of our structures has a lifetime of use, planned or otherwise; the Giza pyramids have been with us for almost five thousand years, while a homeless person in a city park will fashion a shelter that will last one or two days until the cops arrive. Buildings may be modified in any number of ways, but their elemental affiliation usually stays put. The Jefferson Memorial will always evoke metal as long as it stands; if Wright's Robie House didn't feel like the earth element, it wouldn't be the Robie House.

However, environments often change, and this is where energetic adjustments can be made. So in the following discussion, when the elemental balance is unfavorable, follow the "soft" path; don't, for example, tear down the finials, chimney tops, and gable peaks on a Gothic Revival home that happens to be situated next to a pond (a challenging placement because water and fire are in the restraining or destructive cycle, with the fiery home on the receiving end). Rather, make the easier adjustments outdoors, and plant trees next to the pond to establish the nurturing progression of water-wood-fire, and enjoy the much better energy inside and out.

We'll review typical buildings affiliated with each element, and then explore how their environment affects these buildings. While the variety of elemental relationships between site, materials, and environment can seem complex, the underlying pattern is just that of the two cycles of elements promoting and restraining each other. The following list is simplified in that it shows one kind of building in one kind of environment, but the real world is usually much more diverse. Yet even in the most complicated mixture of elements, these basic relations will be at work.

Wood Element Buildings. Look for linear, or

tall and thin design, or conspicuous use of wood materials. These buildings may have multiple pillars or colonnades, as in Greek Revival or plantation-style homes; many modern offices emphasize columns or pillars. Another feature is the use of tall, massive chimneys, often found in Tudor or Georgian style houses; many Tudors also use half-timbered walls, wooden beams, and sometimes even wood shingles. The traditional Japanese home, for example, is built almost entirely of wood. We should bear in mind, however, that in determining an elemental association, shape or form is sometimes more evocative than construction materials. Many tall office towers, for example, built with concrete, an earth-type material, affiliate with the wood element because of their shape. Wood-type buildings give an overall impression of growth, production, and structure.

- When placed in a **wood** environment, such as in a forest or surrounded by other wood element objects, these buildings find a supportive but nondynamic pairing that can help wood-related activities but brings a danger of excess—we've seen earlier some of the problems with dense skyscraper clusters. In other words, too much growth can become a kind of cancer. In homes that are not out of balance, this pairing is ideal for horticulture or for an artist's studio. How to control excess wood? One approach uses metal, which "cuts" or restrains wood; for example, circular shapes in the landscaping and silver, gray, and white colors in the color palette. Another approach uses a small bit of fire to "consume" some of the wood; for example, add a few peaks or sharp corners to the site. Both approaches can be found in the English Jacobethan manor home, the inspiration for the Tudor Revival style, which has yielded some of the lushest domestic gardens in the world.

- In a **fire** environment, perhaps surrounded by prominent spires and pointed roofs on neighboring structures, the wood element building is depleted in some way, since fire consumes wood. In Connecticut, for example, a sea captain built a home with a large pillared façade next to a church dominated by a large steeple. The captain ended his days penniless, although he enriched the community with his heavy spending before going bankrupt. How could he have avoided this pattern, foretold by the Five Element cycle? By using a restraining element: In this case, water, which quenches fire and also nourishes wood. This harmonizing can be seen in old cities, such as Rome and Seville, in the frequent placement of fountains among both spired buildings (fire) and many-pillared colonnades (wood).

- In an **earth** environment, such as on flat plains or among broad, low buildings, the wood structure is stimulated since wood absorbs earth. This is often seen in the Midwest: Some kind of tall tower abruptly rears above the relatively open landscape. An iconic example from the movie *Giant* is the wooden Second Empire–style house with a tall square tower set against the endless prairie. This combination may bring financial success, but one must be careful with relationships based only on the destructive cycle, which are often short-lived. If the environment becomes depleted, like oil wells running dry, the party's over. Many midwestern cities, too, have seen cycles of boom and bust.

- In a **metal** environment, such as one of rounded hills or among rounded arches and domed structures, the wood building is oppressed in some fashion, since metal restrains wood. This is an unusual combination, and hard to find, thus reflecting the unfavorable energy balance. An apparent exception is the thriving city of Hong Kong, whose many skyscrapers rise among dome-like hills. The ch'i flows so well there because of the addition of a strong water element, which is nurtured by metal and in turn nurtures wood; thus the harbor has been prosperous, which in turn stimulates business activities in general. This same potent adjustment, using the nurturing cycle, was mentioned earlier with respect to the Taj Mahal.

- In a **water** environment, close to marshes, rivers, or lakes or at the seaside, or among sinuous or irregular building shapes, wood-element structures are strongly supported, since water promotes wood. In this favorable relationship, business as well as government and creative activities will flourish. Feng shui scholars have carefully placed dynastic Chinese and Japanese imperial pavilions made of wood amid ponds and streams for this very reason.

Fire Element Buildings. These structures feature sharp angles, spires, or strongly pointed roofs. While few of us work or live in a steepled church or something like the Disneyland castle, many office towers have sharply angular designs, such as Pittsburgh's popular neo-Gothic PPG Place or New York's Woolworth Building. Some home types, such as Gothic Revival and other Victorian styles, particularly Queen Anne, feature spires and spiky roofs. Fire-type buildings give an impression of inspiration, aspiration, and transformation.

- When placed in a **wood** environment, fire element buildings and their occupants are stimulated and energized, since wood feeds fire. In other words, an environment of growth promotes inspiration. The structure itself may become more famous than the setting or builder. For example, the Biltmore mansion in a forested park near Asheville, North Carolina, built in the French Gothic Revival style, is the most celebrated mansion in the world.

- In a **fire** environment, fire element buildings enjoy a supportive but possibly volatile relation since there's a danger of excess fire and eventual "burn out." An interesting example of this is King Ludwig of Bavaria's Neuschwanstein Castle, perhaps the most famous castle on earth, rearing up among the sharp peaks and pine forests of the Bavarian Alps. Ludwig's initial plans for his "mountain retreat" grew ever more ambitious, and a four-year construction plan stretched to more than twenty years; additions and modifications spread like wildfire. Eventually the king ran out of money, lost political power as well as his health, and the castle was never finished. Even today, although it is a candidate for one of the seven modern wonders of the architectural world, the vast pile has only fourteen public rooms completed. The usual adjustments used to quench excess fire are to add earth, which will try to preserve inspiration's accomplishments, and an appropriate amount of water to control any, so to speak, runaway flames.

- In an **earth** environment, since fire feeds earth, the fire element building runs the risk of depletion in some way as resources flow out of the building into the surroundings. This isn't always a bad thing, for the building's purpose may be to nurture its environment. Small-town churches, with their steeples the only spire or pointed structure in the area, tend to nourish their community even though the churches often get little material return. We should recall that every situation is different and needs its own evaluation.

- A **metal** environment stimulates the fire element building, as fire melts metal; a danger with such a pairing in the destructive cycle is that the environment can get worn out. For example, a fire element office, like San Francisco's Transamerica pyramid, set on a rounded hillside, may enjoy a period of prosperity and then, as Transamerica

did after its 1970s heyday, lose its support systems. The company was later sold, eventually
broke up, and what remained of Transamerica's
offices exited the pyramid. More recently, as
more tall buildings have gone up in the financial
district—the addition of the wood element—the
popularity of the site has returned.

- In a **water** environment, the fire-type building is
at a disadvantage, since water puts out fire. This
unfavorable placement can dampen home or business activity and take the spark out of the site. As
we saw earlier with Notre Dame in Paris, to remedy such a situation, add the wood element and
establish the generative flow of water-wood-fire.

Earth Element Buildings. Earth-type buildings, with their low profiles, flat roofs, and horizontal
lines, are quite common. Many Americans live in earth-
type homes—the classic ranch style, the boxy Colonial
Revival, the Georgian Revival, the Wright-inspired Prairie style, and the modern International style, to name
a few—and many of us work in mesa-like office parks.

This should be no surprise, as earth is connected to the ideas of preservation and community; moreover, most everyday American architecture is conservative in design and style.

- In a **wood** environment, the earth-type building will be somehow compromised, since wood restrains earth; this draining of energy or material can be slow, as when a tree robs the soil of its nutrients over the years, or occasionally can occur in rapid bursts. A sad example of the latter case is Taliesin, Frank Lloyd Wright's own home in Wisconsin, which witnessed multiple fires,

divorces, and a murder spree, among other trag-
edies. To help this elemental pairing, introduce
the fire element, which feeds on wood and nourishes earth in the creative cycle. For example, if
our low, long office block sits among many trees
or near tall buildings, use fire-type objects in the
environment: pointed shrubbery, lamps, spiked
fences, plants with bright red leaves or flowers, and red objects in the general landscaping.
Wright himself relied on introducing and extending red roofs at Taliesin later in its history, with
good results.

- A **fire** environment feeds and supports the earth-
type building, a favorable pairing for both homes
and offices. One can expect business to grow and
family to thrive. The only problem is that fire
locations are often hard to come by; not everyone
can live in western Colorado or Bavaria, next to
a sharply steepled church, or close to an inspirational publisher. And who would want to live
next to refineries and chemical plants—a siting
that remains excellent for warehouses and storage facilities, however.

- An **earth** environment offers earth buildings stability and conformity, which can become too much of a good thing. There is a danger of complacency and lack of dynamism in this pairing, as businesses so placed can become hide-bound and miss growth opportunities, and home life can become tediously routine and dull. Even strikingly good architecture, like the adobe-inspired work of northern Arizona's Mary Jane Colter, can be ignored or overlooked. The addition of the fire element, and perhaps even water, will stimulate helpful change and activity.

- A **metal** environment is an area marked by rounded hills, circular structures, domes, arches, and metallic materials; it's enriched by the presence of earth-type buildings, since earth nurtures metal but often at the expense of earth. The question is whether this type of change is in line with the purpose of the building; if we're trying to accumulate resources, including money, it's an unfavorable pairing. If our aim is to help the neighborhood or surroundings, including public service or charitable work, it's a good match.

- A **water** environment is in some way harmed—we could say polluted—by earth-type forms, since earth muddies water. This relation will be, for a time, stimulating for the earth building, but it may create negative energies, like resentment from the neighbors. A dramatic example: the immense, warehouse-shaped Château of Versailles, built mainly by King Louis XIV ("The state, that's me," he said) and seat of the French royal court and government from 1672 until 1789, lies in a marshy area surrounded by artificial lakes, ponds, canals, and fountains. Most of these basins did indeed get polluted shortly after they were built; eventually the royal family was driven from power and many of them, such as King Louis XVI, died on the guillotine when the people revolted. The addition of a single prominent dome—introducing the metal element and fostering part of the creative cycle with earth, metal, and water—could have changed the energetic balance completely.[1] Skeptics have scoffed and asked how the shape of this one building could influence the course of world history. The question is wrong; these things are not matters of cause and effect but manifestations—both symbolic and literal—of underlying, connected patterns of change. The eminent psychologist Carl Jung called these esoterically connected patterns synchronicities. Jung had a great appreciation for Taoist thought, as many of his writings attest.

Metal Element Buildings. A rounded dome, a signature shape for these structures, is easily spotted above capitol buildings, temples, and mosques, but it's rarely seen atop either houses or workplaces; however, other strongly rounded architectural elements will also bring a building into the metal category. Arches, for example, dominate the design of homes in the "Richardson Romanesque" (like the Glessner House in Chicago and the American Museum of Natural History) and Spanish Mission/Spanish Revival styles. Metal materials, such as aluminum or bronze sheathing, can also create a metal connection when design or shape isn't more prominent. Metal-affiliated buildings give an overall impression of discrimination, lawfulness, and even purity.

- In a **wood** environment, because metal cuts wood, the metal building becomes some kind of liability to its surroundings. An interesting example of this is found at Thomas Jefferson's Monticello, which is indeed topped by a dome. Its site was originally heavily wooded, but over the years Jefferson was forced to overfarm or liquidate his property as his debts mounted; the building thrived while the land didn't. The elemental tension carries over into the house itself, which has elements of wood (the portico) and earth (brick construction and low, flat wings)—a dynamic setting for a brilliant and often contradictory individual but not an easy place to dwell or raise a (conventional) family. Water would be an effective, soothing elemental addition, as in a reflecting pool or fountain, although a strongly fire-type individual like Jefferson (redheaded, with pointed and ruddy features, inspirational, aggressive, birth-sign in Aries) wouldn't be expected to welcome such an idea.

- In a **fire** environment, the metal-type building is in a disadvantageous setting, since fire melts metal. A helpful adjustment is to introduce the earth element, which is supported by fire and feeds metal in the creative cycle. For example, a Mission style home set in the mountains could add broad, flat terraces; long, low porches; and prominent stucco, stone, or brick exteriors. In a picturesque confirmation of this idea, pioneering Southern California architects such as Irving Gill did this intuitively. A big adjustment may not be practical, however, so we could also introduce the water element, perhaps in the form of a single fountain or pool, to restrain the fire.

- In an **earth** environment, the metal building is nourished and enriched, a favorable pairing for all kinds of office structures as well as for harmonious and refined homes and public spaces. An austerely beautiful example is the Kimbell Museum in Texas from the great architect Louis

Kahn: a symmetrical procession of arches rolling over the Fort Worth prairie.

- In a **metal** environment, the metal element structure is comfortable and neutral, if ultimately understimulated. A possible example would be a Mediterranean-style home set among rolling hills. If the energy of the site seems lackluster, planting trees without pointed tops, like palms, willows, or junipers, will bring some kind of invigorating change; moreover, adding a fountain or pond will improve the site's productivity.

- In a **water** environment, the metal-type building nurtures and enriches the surroundings, including the local community, although it may give too much of itself to stay sound. An archetypical example of this is Vancouver's BC Place: Its white, inflated, perfectly round dome sits on a peninsula among extensive watercourses and faces a channel. BC Place is perennially booked with events, including conventions, shows, and national and Olympic sports, bringing millions of dollars to the city and province, yet manages to lose at least a few million every year. In January 2006 it accidentally tore, deflated, and suffered water damage from rain and snow. More of the earth element in its setting would both support the building and restrain the excessive water energy.

Water Element Buildings. These are often the most interesting to observe, as water buildings can be irregular or somehow formless as well as sinuous and curvy; many Shingle-style homes, with multiple dormers, irregular roof lines, and undulating façades mix together all these features. Offices and factories sometimes have these characteristics in spite of themselves. When a water design is deliberate, as with Frank Gehry's Bilbao Guggenheim Museum, the results can be enchanting. A secondary indication, when form is indistinct, is the use of glass, a water element material, throughout the building. Water element buildings give an overall impression of fluidity, imagination, and mystery.

- In a **wood** environment, a water-type building nurtures its surroundings, since water feeds wood.

If the building feels energetically drained or its resources diminished because of overly strong wood, we could add the metal element to the site, which restrains wood and feeds water. Another option is to introduce the fire element, which stimulates water through the restraining cycle. How does one choose approaches? Along with cost, aesthetics, and practical concerns, the first is quieter, the second more dynamic.

- In a **fire** environment, the water building is stimulated, as water quenches fire. This is a rare pairing; how often do we see a curvaceous, eclectic house set among pointed conifers and sharp peaks? It's an invigorating combination and can be quite stunning; we can find a few examples among the ski lodges the zillionaires have recently built in the Rockies. In cases where the setting is depleted or its energy weakened, introduce the wood element for balance and support.

- In an **earth** environment, the water building is now going to be weakened or inhibited, since earth muddies water. An improvement on this challenging pairing is to use metal, which feeds water and is fed by earth in the creative cycle. If the earthy area is contained, like a plaza, field, or low terrace, we could use a metal sculpture or rounded plants in the landscaping.

- In a **metal** environment, the water-type structure is advantageously placed, as its surroundings will support and stimulate it. An example is the architect Philip Johnson's famous Glass House in the rolling hills outside New Canaan, Connecticut. Although the shape of the building is a simple box, because the exterior is almost all glass the house feels like a giant aquarium. From certain angles or in the right light, even the difference between outside and inside dissolves, a classic water occurrence. This striking residence certainly confirms its creator's imagination, whimsy, and wit.

- In a **water** environment, the water building can feel much at home and can certainly thrive, but there is a danger that the one element is overemphasized. A telltale sign is too much change and irregularity in the activities of the building, communication without substance, or just plain confusion. Adding the metal element to the surroundings will create stability and clarity.

Multi-element Buildings

The above survey is simplified, as I mentioned; many structures combine influences from different elements, creating a richer set of relationships. For example, a French Provincial– (or Normandy-) style home with tall chimneys and half-timbering (wood element) may also have high, pointed, multiple dormers and roofs (fire element). A Colonial Revival home, built low and relatively flat-roofed (earth), may feature a prominent arch over the entry (metal) or a rounded Palladian window in its center. There are ten possible combinations like these, and if you include homes with *three* elements, you get another ten possibilities. For example, some Victorian houses have pillars or a tower (wood), arches and a domed cupola (metal), and spiked roofs and pointed gables (fire). Some "postmodern" homes have curved sections and lots of glass (water), round windows (metal), and a low profile (earth). And so on. In the same way, many environments show a combination of elements, such as a water-wood site that has ponds as well as trees. Three elements involved in a site are not at all unusual: rolling hills, streams, and mountains in the landscape evoke metal, water, and fire, respectively. So, with at least twenty times twenty, meaning four hundred, more possible combinations, how do we know what to harmonize and balance?

The answer is simple, although what's simple is not always easy to do: We feel what's going on at the site, then the principles at work and the sensation of the elements supporting and restraining one another will become clear. A huge case in point is New York's Cathedral of St. John the Divine, which suffered an unfortunate blending of elements—a sad contrast to the earlier-mentioned Notre Dame in Paris. The placement of a "temporary" brick dome seventy years ago over the center crossing of this many-spired and pinnacled Gothic church so disturbed the balance (metal and fire are in the destructive cycle) that ever since, this cathedral has been plagued by interminable construction delays, fire, loss of property and patronage, and near bankruptcy. So how could the church officials have foreseen this? We

need to feel how change, Yin/Yang, and creation and destruction all progress. After spending time at the site, meditate and reflect, bringing all observations of ch'i (as presented in the previous chapter) together with the elemental aspects to form a unique perception of the site. As much as we seek its character, we also let it reveal itself to us.

Walking the Walk

Here's a chance to really work those memory and imagination muscles. Using all the spaces you've experienced in your travels, work, home life, and so on, jot down in your notebook an example of a wood-affiliated space or building in each of the different elemental settings. Then move on to fire buildings, then earth, metal, and water. You'll need to assemble about two dozen examples, and some might be hard to find, such as a metal building in a fire setting. At that point, give it a rest and come back later; some recollection from youth or a forgotten trip will usually come to the rescue. The gung-ho can hit the Internet.

CHAPTER SIX

Creating Good
Energy Inside Home
and Office

learly, being indoors and being out-
doors feels different, but there's more
to the story than most of us realize. As
we've seen, a site and its buildings are
energetically bound together, and this
interaction influences the activities of the inhabitants
whether they're inside or out. Whatever vital forces and
patterns—ch'i and Five Elements—we find outside
a structure don't just disappear when we walk inside.
Rather, they continue to manifest themselves by influ-
encing events and people inside. To take an obvious
example, working in a ranch-style office on the Great
Plains will have a very different effect on us than will

working in a skyscraper in a crowded city. So, having considered some of the effects of the outer environment, we now look at some energies and types of changes created by uniquely indoor conditions. For example, there might be a dead end in the hallway outside your office, and regardless if you're in a high-rise or out on the plains, we need to make sure that vital energy, ch'i, doesn't stagnate in this dead space. None of the principles and practices that we've used before will change, but there will be new circumstances requiring new applications, which the rest of this chapter will explore.

Getting Started: The Bigger Picture

Let's begin by working with a space that's accessible and right at hand: Your home or office is fine. First, find or draw a floor plan or plans of your space and trace the flow of activity throughout the building, from the main entrance or entrances to all the exits or other doors. If there's only one door, as in many apartments and offices, there will still be a circulation pattern. Recall everyone who uses the space, and for what purpose.

Also feel/think about how things and people, ourselves included, move through the rooms—cultivating good ch'i requires understanding *how things move* just as much as knowing *what is moving*. For example, is there a room or area that makes us want to hurry away or rush past it? We also need to ask how we'd *like* people to move in a particular space. If the site is a shop, store, or room where sales are made, we should be enticed to move around freely and comfortably, savoring one exciting presentation after another. On the other hand, in an office focused on communication, such as one in an advertising agency, smart design usually emphasizes rapid, efficient, and open lines of access. Whatever the pace and style of human movement in a given location, the basic ideas of good flow remain simple: Avoid congestion and constriction, such as cluttered and closed-off spaces; natural light should be able to reach every room; and fresh, clean air should ventilate all areas. We also need to think about completions; every activity, from manufacturing a component to writing a story to washing the dishes, needs to cease smoothly, clean up easily, drain quickly, and leave quietly.

Speaking of cleaning, to help find areas deficient in vital energy, note where dust settles in a smooth, undisturbed coating. While storage centers, like book shelves and DVD/CD racks, can be expected to get a little accumulation now and then, there are many instances where you can ask "the dust question": Can I get rid of this (fill in the blank: chair, table, whatever) and reduce clutter if all this thing does is collect dust? Seasonal items, rarely used objects, mementoes, and hand-me-downs, such as Christmas wreaths and your partner's slide trombone, should be put in storage, or, if applicable, given a new home where the item is really needed and will be used. If we have closets, attics, or basements, or rent storage space, let's make optimal use of them: While keeping access sensible, fill them to the brim. The goal for all the other (nonstorage) spaces is simple: Every object and every area has use, and nothing gathers dust, at least unintentionally. And herein lies an opportunity for a distinctly Taoist practice: We may intentionally want some areas to just sit there, as it were.

Is there really a practical use for some kind of "useless" space? Well, what good is an empty cup? Most homes and offices need to have "empty" areas where it seems like nothing happens, yet the space is pregnant with possibility. As with Tao itself, the unseen is paramount. We need space where something new can appear, that can absorb and cushion the unexpected and provide a refuge for whatever isn't immediately apparent. For example, a friend unexpectedly gave a neighbor a bicycle when the neighbor least expected such a useful gift; serendipitously, because this neighbor's apartment had a bit of seemingly useless "breathing room," the bike created no disruption in the living space. It was as if that bit of empty space was waiting for a wonderful partner. We also need space into which we're drawn to reflect, to meditate, to use silence to find where we really are. What could be more practical than that? So this "useless" area may be the soul of the building, so to speak, and the most important sector of all. We'll look into extending this idea in more detail later.

Balance, Flow, and Authenticity—Again

Recall that well-flowing energy is balanced energy—we don't want the opposite challenge from stagnation, which is frantic ch'i. Too much "spinning one's wheels" can be worse than vegetating. If dust clues us in to areas with too little vital energy, too much wear or trails of debris, like those found next to busy streets, will show excessive activity. So think about slowing things down in those spots. Here are some examples where we often have to improve energetic flow, whether it's too sparse or too abundant:

- Doors and windows shouldn't line up on a straight axis in any rooms where people spend time, because ch'i will move too quickly through these spaces; aligned openings make these rooms feel like hallways or galleries, and people won't want to stay there, let alone sit down and relax. On the other hand, effective waiting areas and transit spaces will emphasize this plan—New York's Grand Central Terminal is crisscrossed by traffic straightaways. (Contrast this with Washington's sluggish-feeling Union Station, which pulls tourists into a bazaarlike maze of commercial stands, stores, cafés, and outlets.)

By the same token, front and rear doors shouldn't line up in homes or offices if we want ch'i to stay; if there's a transverse hall bisecting the building, guests who've just entered will feel, often unconsciously, that they've already been "shown the door." If we discover such a problem, how do we slow down this flow?

- Since structural changes can be expensive, screen off one of the doors or the less important window, or use other kinds of partitions creatively—here's an opportunity for harmonious design to assert itself as well as an additional chance to improve the elemental balance in some way. For example, one person's front door and entry hall lined up directly with the living room and main window, which made the living room feel like an extension of the hall. This living room also had a pronounced lack of the water element. So we placed a carved wooden screen behind an indoor fountain just inside the room, which actually caught three birds in one net: The elements in the room became balanced, the ch'i in the home slowed down, and whole area became more sensorially rich and elegant. If there is a budget for structural changes, add a small porch, vestibule, glassed-in breezeway, or conservatory to ease the flow in the same way that a curving entry-path helps slow the energy in an outdoor landscape. Our imaginations can really begin to take flight when we start to combine and play a bit with these ideas.

- Stairways that face outer doors just beg energy to fly out. Even when they face inner doors, they can bring too much ch'i to the room behind the door. A more optimal situation places stairways adjacent to, or turning into, the flow pattern, but not aligning with it directly. Again, moving a stairway can be prohibitively expensive, but varieties of hall partitions can slow down or baffle the rushed ch'i; some practitioners have found placing plants and sculptures in the passage to be helpful.

- Rooms over a garage are a bugaboo in traditional feng shui because of the fear, imagined or not, of stagnant and harmful ch'i in the vicinity. Such fear is unnecessary. To begin with, a garage needs to be uncluttered, bright, and well-ventilated because of the occasional smells, leaks, and drippings, despite our best efforts at regular cleanings; moreover, we should never run a car indoors because it produces toxic carbon monoxide, which is colorless and odorless. Having achieved a healthful energy, a garage can now be an asset to the property, not a liability, and there may be opportunities to create mixed-used spaces even though there's a car below, next to, or even above us (such as a carport above a cellar).

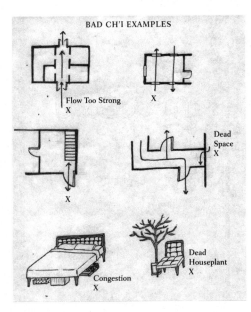

All of our spaces are valuable; to get the most from a garage with extra room, set clear boundaries and plan for possible activities. For example, one family got rid of one of their two cars and now uses the space for a home winemaking center. Another popular mixed-use garage plan features a home craft area or a wood and metal shop. These will need heat in cold weather, so add extra insulation to save on heating bills—and insulation is a smart thing to use between floors if there are activities above or below the garage. Garage space is usually a storage area, affiliated with the earth element, and there's no reason why rooms around it can't harmonize with it in the elemental sense. To cite an obvious example, many kinds of social activities (water) will not feel right near the garage. Indeed, if the garage is active and noisy, especially at night, certainly don't put a bedroom above it. Intelligent use of the space we have remains our guiding light.

- Blocked or congested energy, even "dead ch'i," can occur wherever there are closed-off, isolated, or remote spaces. These spots can be natural, like an elephant's graveyard, but we usually don't want them in a home. Ever find a dead mouse behind

Grandpa's old bureau in the basement? There's our clue. Give the bureau to a charity, get a tax deduction, and reclaim that space for the living. And while the upper half of rooms rarely develop these cul-de-sacs—unless there are unused ducts and hidden recesses—near the floor it can get hairy, literally. Beds and desks, where many of us spend half of our adult lives, should be open in front and to the sides so that air can circulate through and around them. Resist the temptation to store stuff underneath them!

- Search interior areas for, and remove or remedy, any broken objects, sick plants, unpleasant or ugly objects, and vaguely threatening things like exposed, overly sharp corners, which some Chinese practitioners call "poison arrows." Get rid of any household or business articles that bother you, like that paperweight from an office gig that ended up miserably; perverse energy comes in many forms and flavors, and if it can't be removed easily, use one of the adjustments discussed later. Now let's consider in more detail the "what" of interior ch'i.

Keep Asking: Who or What Is Circulating?

The energy flow in our rooms includes not only the movement of light, air, water, and other nonsentient things but also the actions of our family, colleagues, friends, and all the other people in our lives. Without delving into family psychology, here are a few recommendations on cultivating good family energy (these can apply to many office situations, which tend to have some kind of family pattern to them):

- All members of the family, from age five or so on up, need their own inviolate private space somewhere, which the others of us know and respect. Whether it's rational or not, psychologically speaking we need some kind of refuge. Furthermore, it's a good question to ask if this private space needs much in the way of personal paraphernalia. Few of us contemporary Americans, with our attachments to various kinds of stuff, can say, like the ancient sages whom Lao Tsu called seekers of truth, that we "leave no traces."

The beginning of a powerful personal meditation can be found in asking the question whether life would be better off if this object, arrangement, look, or attachment were to just move on.

- On the other hand, communal spaces generally need to be free of personal objects. All those sharing in family benefits also share in family responsibilities; all members, equally and together, must fight the never-ending war on clutter, congestion, and bad ch'i. If the leaders of the family, business, company, or team take it upon themselves to see that everyone feels that they have a stake in maintaining and even improving the general energy, harmony has a better chance to prevail. Mom's tennis racket, Dad's fishing rod, or the manager's golf clubs don't belong in the entry hall. Small things add up; the boss shouldn't wonder why one day the most capable new employee quits, as parents shouldn't have to ask why junior lives in Singapore and never calls. Continual, vigilant attention is a small price to pay for keeping everyone working together; as Lao Tsu wrote, "Prepare for problems before they become problems; achieve what's great by starting small" (*Tao Te Ching,* Verse 63). It's necessary that human organizations understand laws and regulations, and yet realizing that that which inspires a good rule is greater than the rule itself. In just that sense, for example, communal spaces that serve the group best may not always be clear, open, or free of one person's control. If the company kitchen is a mess, someone must initially commit to straighten and organize things; if others don't like it, they can get involved, constructively. It's rare, however, not to see someone's ego get attached to the space, and then negativity can easily develop. These situations, the most difficult of all to clear up, should be seen as a question of what do we really need, right now? Finally, let's not forget the free, available help from the invisible "beyond," the cosmic but hidden way in which our intuition can see or hear the answer. As Lao Tsu wrote, "The family that cultivates Tao abounds in virtue."

- Next, who visits your home, and what kind of experience do your guests have? Nothing ratch-

ets up the energy of a residence or business like
interesting, stimulating visitors. Throughout the
ages, great homes were organized around enter-
taining, from Roman Emperor Hadrian's villa
to the Elizabethan Hardwick Hall to Marjorie
Post's Hillwood Mansion in Washington, D.C.
Treatises on how to give successful dinner parties were written more than 3,500 years ago during China's Shang Dynasty. Without going into
another treatise, here are some suggestions for
cultivating better guest ch'i: Don't always rely
on the same old, same old. A flow of new faces
is good, balanced with old friends, of course, so
invite new acquaintances over—there's nothing to
lose by networking and much to gain. *The Wall
Street Journal* found in a survey that 72 percent
of higher-level corporate jobs were filled through
personal acquaintance and word-of-mouth references. We should bring a variety of people into the
home; our understanding of personal energy—
personal ch'i—as well as the Five Elements can
help. A party filled with strong fire types—people
trying to illuminate or inspire us, so to speak—
would be disastrous, since everyone would want

to talk, with no one to listen. Or maybe you've been to a gathering where earth predominated (a focus on preservation), and the only thing the guests felt like doing was to sit around and stare at the aquarium. Even so, there might be a time and place when that would be appropriate, like a gathering of Cleveland sports fans after yet another missed championship opportunity. But in general, let's go for balance and variety in our guest lists and not be afraid to take some risks, like inviting the woman down the street with the green Mohawk. These folks may be a little provocative or, alternately, intimidated, but we all need the kind of growth that interaction with different types can bring. No less a political genius than Abraham Lincoln appointed to his cabinet wildly diverging, difficult, yet talented and stimulating individuals, which helped him immensely to save the Union. As for making our guests comfortable as well as bringing out their best sides, we can again take our cue from Lincoln, who never lost his self-assurance and sincerity. Thus our rooms must show our own sense of identity, our own ideas, tastes, history, feelings, and so forth, rather than be a formulaic showplace that "puts on the dog." As Lao Tsu wrote, "Act without 'acting'; work without being busy, flavor without seasoning, magnify by lessening, repay malice with kindness" (*Tao Te Ching*, Verse 63). If that isn't a recipe for putting on a wonderful, successful party, what is?

The Personal Side of Adjusting Inside Ch'i

We must circulate through our homes and work spaces, too. How we feel and function can be improved by studying ourselves in action. Take height, for example. Until recently, thanks to good nutrition and health care, Americans were the tallest people of any nationality; now it's the Dutch (as reported by Paul Krugman in *The New York Times*, June 15, 2007). Even today, many men and women top out at six feet or more (about one in five men, according to government surveys), which gives them a reach of more than seven and a half feet—the ceiling height of many modern offices and houses. Especially in large rooms, this feels oppressive;

moreover, many doorways and stairway lintels barely clear six feet, causing head bangs and even injuries. Talk about bad ch'i for tall folks! They should consider finding an older, high-ceilinged home and have that infernal drop ceiling removed from their office. It's far better to open up that space than to hide pipes and ducts behind ugly acoustical tile. A person's "kinesthetic space," the sort of spherically shaped field around our bodies (recall Leonardo da Vinci's famous sketch) defined by how we move, like reaching, striding, stretching, jumping, sitting, and so on, increases its volume by about four *cubic feet* for every additional inch of height. A petite five-foot-five former gymnast simply cannot have the same living scale as a six-five former hoops player. Chairs, desks, beds, shelving and other storage systems, picture and screen heights, windows, sight lines in general—the list is huge—need to take this scale into account to be healthy and supportive; most furniture manufacturers are still woefully in the dark about this. For example, when we find a closed-off or dead area, let's think before throwing a mirror up on the back wall. While a mirror still happens to be an excellent remedy for dead ch'i, what are we going to see in it—the ceiling, the floor, or our knees? A mirror's effectiveness is maximized at eye level, which will be different for each occupant. Yes, some remedies, like custom desks and chairs, can be expensive, but we must pay attention to energetic configurations—the feng shui—and let them help us live in our bodies better; there's nothing more valuable than our health. A lanky entrepreneur waited almost five years for a new recycling business to take off, and his first purchases when the cash flow finally began were a new widescreen computer and a huge ergonomic chair; his excruciating headaches and neck pains soon disappeared.

The challenge of low ceilings brings up an old-time bugaboo: exposed beams overhead. There is a traditional maxim that wooden beams harm our ch'i, especially if we sleep or work under them. Well, if one is a strongly earth or water person or someone focused on preserving or dissolving something, an overpowering symbol of growth above us, even if it's unconscious, might well be disturbing. The key question is how high above us the beams are placed; if the ceiling is high to begin with, our energy can be little affected. If the ceiling is low, we should move our bed or desk if we feel any kind of "oppression," like we're in some kind of cage. Water pipes and electrical conduits are a more serious matter, since they both can carry electromagnetic fields that can be subtly disturbing, according to some scientific studies. Indeed, traditional feng shui has long asserted that we shouldn't work, sleep, or sit near running water for any length of time. If the headboard to the bed is next to a wall enclosing pipes, move it out even a few inches and also place something substantial on the wall, like a painting or large photograph, design permitting. This last point brings up an important question: How to integrate the material objects in our rooms with other elements like use, form, color, light, style, and so forth. The next chapter explores how the five changes or elements can help us continue to improve interior energy, but first a few more important aspects of indoor ch'i must be considered:

Ch'i on Even Smaller Scales—with Large Consequences

Big consequences because this work is Taoist, naturally! The placement of beds and work surfaces, like desks, where we spend about half of our adult lives, has received much modern feng shui attention.

Many people have heard of the "commanding posi-

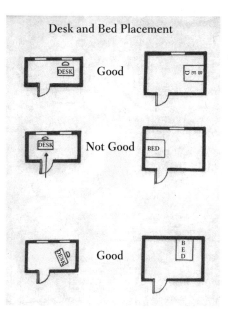

tion" even if they know nothing else about feng shui, and there is certainly good theory and solid experience behind it (see the diagram above). The commanding position requires that your bed or desk face the main entrance to the room, where much of the room's ch'i enters, while at the same time not lying in the direct path of that ch'i— the same principle discussed in Chapter Four. There is a definite advantage to seeing who's entering the room; moreover, placing one's back to the door unsettles some of us psychologically. But as with all such considerations, they don't exist outside one's own unique context. Recall the fellow in Chapter Four who felt that his sight line over New York harbor was too enriching not to enjoy directly. If you're uncertain about desk and bed placement, by all means experiment. Moving the bed is nothing compared to, say, knocking a wall down or changing your address. Your intuition will tell you how this test is working; the change may be worth it even if you feel something's being sacrificed. And later you may feel different and move things around again. To paraphrase the philosopher Heraclitus, we can never sit at the same desk twice.

Many folks ask about the use of spiritual or religious images in various rooms. For a truly sensitive, attuned person, every object is in some way spiritual. Look at what's around us. Here's a table that was made in an Amish village; that blanket came from a pow-wow in South Dakota. This lamp belonged to someone's beloved uncle; that bookcase survived a college dorm, and so on. Belongings have a spectrum of history and significance, with varying degrees of emotional intensity. A chair we just bought doesn't have the feel of something we've lived with and liked for many years. All the same, specifically religious things should be treated with another level of respect. Buddha statues, to pick a common example, should not be mere decoration; they should be placed in important locations and used by the owner in some kind of meditation, even if it's rarely practiced or brief. Similarly, the currently hip and coyly fashionable use of Roman Catholic imagery in interior design, such as the Sacred Heart of Jesus and Novena candles, is inappropriate. From the point of view of traditional feng shui, a crucifix, showing a man (or God) dying in agony, is so powerfully disruptive of ch'i that it should be hung only with sincerest piety and reverence. If someone wants to put one on the wall "just because Aunt Maria did," it's also inappropriate. Hanging calligraphy of Gospel teachings would suffer this casual approach much more constructively. Some images, like Maneki Neko, the little Japanese welcoming cat figurine, are meant to be mundane, nonspiritual, and business-minded. On this subject, people ask if other traditions can blend with feng shui practices. Experience has shown that, with an open mind, wonderful synergies can be realized. For example, someone who studies Hinduism wanted to place a Ganesh statue (Ganesh is a Hindu god, Shiva's son, with an elephant head in one of his forms, who presides over fortunate beginnings) in the entry of her yoga studio. She felt all the energies to be encouraging, including the perceived attitude of Ganesh himself, and went ahead. It couldn't have hurt, as her yoga practice blossomed. Nevertheless, in the blending of traditions one must proceed as if handling enriched uranium. Given this caution, one may go ahead and get a glimpse of the Sufi poet Rumi's vision of endless invisible ladders "reaching step by step to the summit of Heaven; a different ladder for every path, a different path for every group."

Ch'i, Pets, and Plants

> In the home of the future . . . our rooms will descend close to the ground, and the garden will become an integral part of the house. The distinction between the indoors and the out-of-doors will disappear. The walls will be few, thin, and removable. All rooms will become parts of an organic unit instead of being small separate boxes with peep-holes.
>
> —RUDOLF SCHINDLER, ARCHITECT[1]

Having other creatures around will influence the energy of any space. For many people, having animal companions in the home increases their own vital energy. Houseplants can be subtly enriching, and arrangements of flowers have an undeniably potent effect on any room. A whole book could be written on creating these kinds of environmental harmony. To generalize, some of us are dedicated plant or pet people, and some of us just have no interest in those things. For those in the middle, here are some considerations. In spaces where there's not enough activity, not enough movement, healthy pets increase ch'i. What's more, as animals function more on the physical and emotional levels, many have an intuition when a location's energy needs to be zinged or quieted. Stereotypically, big dogs up the energy a lot, small dogs less, cats even less. (But whoever has met a truly crazy cat knows otherwise!) Caged animals like birds, hamsters, and turtles have a minimal effect on ch'i. However, a singing canary or talking parakeet can feel omnipresent; moreover, the cage strongly symbolizes discipline and confinement. Symbolic associations add an important dimension to the pet's space, from the mysterious aura given by many cat breeds to the sweetness of rabbits to the allure of snakes, so we need to ask: What images does my pet project? Since the Chinese traditionally associate goldfish with wealth, for example, they tend to be oversubscribed as feng shui adjustments. Nevertheless, aquarium fish, the quietest of pets, can have a great visual impact; the dullest-looking room can come to life with a few brightly colored fish. Make sure, though, you're not supporting trade in endangered species, as many brilliant tropical fish have become.

Speaking of aquariums, let's be clear about one thing: Pets are not mere accessories to a space or building. Pets are invariably a commitment, sometimes huge, of time and resources. They must be kept in the best of health, physically and emotionally, for a house with the healthiest energy can be upended in one day by a sick dog. A pet must be wanted, loved, and cared for if it's going to have a positive impact on the home or business. We must be conscious of the bargain, so to speak; the right dog, for example, can fill our space with non-judgmental affection and ground it in a simpler, more physical, and feeling-centered way of life—as long as she's given the right food, shelter, veterinary care, daily exercise, and mindful attention. We must be mindful as well of the pet's life cycle; the bounciest Jack Russell or the sprightliest spaniel will some day be slow, arthritic, and needing extra care. Dealing with a failing animal is not the same as pruning a perennial or replacing a brown ficus. Are we ready for these changes?

It's a very big question, not to be taken lightly. Gone are the days in early America, which was ninety percent rural, when our property had far more animals than people. Horses and oxen worked the fields, dogs guarded flocks and buildings, cats killed rodents, hens laid eggs, and all kinds of ducks, geese, cows, and goats—at first adorable babies, now accessible only in petting zoos—matured and ended up as dinner. Animal energy surrounded us, and thus we were more in touch with life, death, and what philosophers called the Great Chain of Being. That is to say, closer to Tao. Today swatting a fly or walking (quickly) past a lobster tank is the closest we get to the Wild Kingdom. What in our inner life has thus been lost?

Taking care of houseplants is an easier consideration, as some require minimal maintenance—a little water and sunlight from time to time—and can add quite a lot of good energy to any space. On the level of chemistry, plants take in carbon dioxide and release oxygen; some even filter impurities in the air. There are literally thousands of plant species that can be cultivated in most rooms, and our sense of element balance (see below) will help us choose most effectively. Above all, make sure that all plants are healthy; in terms of care, they can be a surprising microcosm of our relations to other living things. As many gardeners know, plants are like people. So know your plants and do right by them. When a room or area is severely depleted of vital energy, you may want to try a *tsuboniwa*. This is a Japanese word meaning "small garden," in the sense of a little pocket of greenery and related objects tucked away in a limited space; indoors, *tsuboniwa* is a strong and beautiful way to improve the energy in almost any room

even when it's the size of a closet. All we need are a few appropriate healthy plants, which will depend on the available light (which can be augmented with discreet artificial sources); gravel or river stones to fill out the dedicated area; perhaps some larger rocks; maybe a small basin of water or sculpture; and we have a striking oasis that can pump lots of ch'i into the most arid sites.

Ch'i, Sounds, and Smells

Speaking of canaries and goats, smell is an important aspect of interior energy, as is ambient sound. The most impressive-looking space fails if it smells off or has unpleasant acoustics, while the plainest room can feel great because of wonderful odors and sounds. Olfactory and acoustical environments are a huge subject, and again I'll have to be brief; detailed discussions for the more advanced student are at last becoming more common.

Biologists are discovering more and more significant powers of odors, which can influence choice of mate, mood, and memory function—something perfumers and novelists have known for ages. Many Americans have been brainwashed by the deodorizing industry that all smells are bad, hence the common put-down "it smells," as if having any odor whatsoever is a crime. Let's wake up: Everything alive, and many things not, have an olfactory signature, which makes as much sense to ignore as never looking at something. Indeed, a dog can find one person faster in a stadium of 50,000 by sniffing than can several detectives searching with photographs. So we should tune in to this whole world, this sensorium, which may be the easiest and strongest way to improve a room's energy.

Perfumers identify three traditional groups of fragrances: *floral*—a huge category containing everything from iris to lavender to rose to violet; *oriental*—including spices, musk, vanilla, and exotic resins; and *woody*—examples are cedar, pine, patchouli, vetiver, and sandalwood, among many others. To these groups, modern fragrance experts add citrus, moss, grass, leather, and the massive herbal category. And as these odors are for typical colognes, we've barely sniffed out a fraction of what's out there, such as countless food, animal, and synthetic scents. The use of scent is likewise potentially huge; here are a few examples: A space that just witnessed some kind of agitation (like an argument or an unsuccessful meeting) can be soothed with lavender, sandalwood, bergamot, or cedar. Because scent has such a powerful subliminal effect on us, a little goes a long way; be very conservative in using it. If a room has stagnant ch'i, liven it up with jasmine, patchouli, frankincense, or rose. Or if the energy is hyperactive, slow it with Roman chamomile, ylang-ylang, neroli, or geranium. Some of these common scents (common to the perfumer) may sound exotic—ylang-ylang??—so here's a chance to learn new things, which is good ch'i for the mind; there are ways to do this listed below. These scents can be diffused through burning, as when incorporated in incense, spraying dilute essential oils, evaporation from a basin, or through swatches. Be careful in working with essential oils, as they are highly concentrated and, like anything with extreme power, potentially harmful. So dilute them by mixing in tiny amounts with another, neutral oil, such as a mineral or vegetable oil, called a carrier; the mix will be safe.

Sound also can instantly shift the ch'i in any space. Ever enjoy a sumptuous meal in a stunning setting, only to have a crying child intrude like a toothache? If scent has been an oft-neglected component of interior energy, acoustic influences are perhaps even more ignored. But thanks to modern electronics, including computers and laptops with fine audio systems, any room's ch'i can be adjusted with minimal fuss and expense. Sure, a real fountain or real wind chimes (beloved in traditional feng shui) have that "something extra" that analog systems can always hold over digital imitations, but how are we going to activate those chimes—run a fan behind them all day? So don't rule out using an audio disc if you don't have a caged singing cricket (and you'll save on dicing apples and carrots, too, for the voracious critters). As with smell, these contributions are potent, so set them barely above audible: A nightingale across the yard is heaven; one next to our desk is hell. So here, again briefly, are some common popular sound adjustments:

- When the room's energy is a little too low, many bird songs, cicadas, or other animal sounds are a great nudge up. So are mixes of forest and lake sounds, although there are versions that are calming as well. If close to the sea, try whale songs. In an office, the energy can be brought up nicely and unobtrusively with an "office mix" evoking distant printers, copiers, and low conversation. A light street-sound mix can work in both home and office, but a beach mix, delightful at home, can distract in the office. When the room needs a jolt, a busy street- or jungle-sound mix can really push it, although, to reiterate, the volume should be quite low.

- When the interior energy is too high, sound loops of a gentle rainfall, waves lapping the shore, an easy breeze through leaves and trees, and a burbling stream (similar to an indoor fountain) are wonderfully calming. So are certain animal sounds, like loon calls or the above-mentioned cricket, among other sleepy-time associations. The tick-tock of an old-fashioned pendulum clock soothes many people, but loud chimes can announce the passing hours too strenuously. White noise, which covers the whole spectrum of tones, has been found to calm medical patients. Specific sounds, like those of running water or a crackling wood fire, have a Five Element effect on the room (the next chapter is all about such effects), which must be taken into account as well. For example, the choice of wood or metal chimes in the sound environment can affect this balance.

Here's an aside about "elevator music," ambient music, and Muzak: Authentic or genuine music is composed or performed to be heard with full attention. It's a disservice to the listener to have music as a background to work or some other primary activity.

Better not to use music at all; for that twenty-second elevator ride, one of the loops mentioned above is great. There are also specifically ambient compositions that use electronic drones and harmonious overtones to create an auditory texture similar to the natural sounds listed above; these loops are not music in the sense that Beethoven, Mingus, and Soundgarden are music. But before stowing away your headset, continuous, repetitive activities such as jogging and washing the dishes certainly allow us full musical attention.

Walking the Walk

Grab that notebook and begin making a list of scents that are pleasing or enjoyable; try to recall at least a few, such as the shore after a summer rain, a hike through a pine forest, or Mom's tomato sauce slowly cooking on the stove. Interesting, isn't it, how emotions pervade these olfactory memories. Using the "mind's nose," like working with visual imagination or the mind's eye, may feel strange at first, so don't worry—a little practice will work wonders. When your scent list has some heft, consider what kind of effect each smell would have on the energy of some important rooms, both at home and at work. For more in-depth work, it's often necessary to go to a store with an extensive cologne and perfume selection and learn their various components and mixtures. There are usually lots of samples in atomizers; be prepared to wipe the wrist and forearm clean several times.

Working with sound in the environment can begin similarly: Recall five places or five events that were exceptionally wonderful or stimulating, like a visit to Hawaii, Alaska, or the Caribbean; a retreat next to a mountain lake; that sort of thing. List some of the pleasing or interesting sounds that you heard or associate with this event. We can also try to figure out what sounds affect us in different ways; we can use the Five Elements as an organizer: What sounds make us active, calm, attentive, dreamy, and so on? Imagine the effect of sounds that evoke wood, fire, and water; metallic sounds; and earthy sounds like clay and stone. Consider their effect, at low levels, on various rooms. It's also enlightening to survey friends and family as to how some of these sounds affect them—the results may be surprisingly diverse, and they show us yet again how environmental work must always be individualized.

CHAPTER SEVEN

The Five Elements and Indoor Patterns of Change

I n an active, healthy home or office, change, whether gradual or sudden, small or large, is inevitable. Photos or pictures may lose their appeal; chairs, sofas, and rugs wear out; things break; a client or family member wants a more comfortable or inspiring feel to a room. Rather than resisting the natural process of change, let's embrace it and use it to further our goals. And while this section is concerned with material things, always think of the energies behind the things, the reason for their being. Because most rooms have distinct functions, the main section of this chapter will look at each of them in light of the Five Elements. As with building exteriors, we'll use those elements as particular emphases or resonances—growth, inspiration, preservation, discrimination, dissolution—to harmonize interior space. First, however, to clear the air on an important question:

Should We Bother with Interior Design?

At its best, what's called "style" uses cultural, historical, and artistic contexts within which we can express our tastes, ideas, and life concerns. It should be a tool for our own creativity and self-expression, not an alien pattern imposed on our rooms from somewhere else. And it should work with the room in an elemental sense. For example, Shaker furniture might appeal to us because of its spare simplicity. Yet outfitting the entire living room as a complete Shaker reproduction sends the message that we either want to live in a museum, or even a sex-segregated commune featuring vigorous dancing in daily church services (the origin of the word *Shaker*), or that we simply lack imagination and ideas—hence the use of other people's ideas. On the other hand, blending pieces of Shaker furniture in an individualized way can make sense; they have a strong earth quality that can balance a room filled with irregular shapes, or lots of glass—in other words, a water-dominated room (earth restrains water)—or work synergistically with metal or round objects and activities emphasizing discrimination (earth nurtures metal). The degree to which this blending works is up to us; if the living room is frequently filled with people watching football over pizza and beer, maybe not at all. In a certain bank's corporate offices, it was a great success. We try to make sure that the furnishings and interiors not only provide a purely physical fit, but we select pieces that also speak to us both emotionally and logically, almost as friends with whom we'll want to spend lots of time. Thus style in the sense of Style-with-a-capital-S becomes a secondary concern at most. That said, the more advanced student may want to pursue Five Element connections to established styles; Appendix I provides a more detailed guide to interior functions, period materials, and stylized looks.

The Elements of Interior Function and Form

Other things being equal, ever notice how working on a creative project or a demanding bit of homework is easier at the kitchen table? And how the same work can feel more difficult at a library? In the language of the Five Elements, the fire nature of the kitchen is congenial to inspiration and transformation, while the earth nature of most libraries, whose function/character is storage, restraint, and conservatism, is not. Successful harmonizing of interior environmental energies requires accepting the essential natures of different spaces, be they at home or at work. Considerations of looks, style, design, and so forth follow from these basic natures, not the other way around. So let's visit a number of different rooms to see how the elements function.

Entry Areas. This is normally the first indoor area that we and our friends, relatives, and colleagues experience; first impressions register strongly, even if unconsciously. This space is affiliated with the water element, for it naturally emphasizes flow and movement to somewhere else; it's not a space where we do things or repose for any length of time. It's no coincidence, either, that water (element) is connected to issues of self-identity. So whether we have a grand entry hall with a multistory staircase or a humble four-by-four vestibule, we should place something here—some kind of art, picture, sculpture, photo, or whatever, that represents for us the spirit of the house or of our business. Quiet is better than showy (think of Tao); for example, a large, glossy, posed family portrait from a professional studio is not as authentic as a piece of pottery made by one of the family members. Also think of things to make your guests feel welcome: Plants and flowers are terrific, although too many bright, colorful, eye-catching fiery things will feel weakened or out of place in a water environment. On the other hand, some entries connect directly to a waiting or reception area, and the energy changes. Thus it's no surprise that the word *foyer* is derived from the word *focus*, which means "hearth" in Latin. In olden times it was much appreciated when cold or sodden travelers could warm themselves by a cheery fire near the entry. Frank Lloyd Wright revived the use of a centrally placed foyer fireplace, framed through a low entry, as a potent symbol of the whole house, and it makes great elemental logic: His earth-affiliated homes

(Prairie style, for example) are nurtured by fire. FLW certainly wasn't the only inspired—and well-funded—architect to have re-created the symbolic passage from the dark waters of a constraining womb to the light and openness of day; examples in temples, palaces, courts, capitols, and stadiums abound.

When combining elements, many kinds of entries traditionally make use of objects connected to wood, such as columns, seen in neoclassic porticoes, which works, since water feeds wood. Arches and domes over entries, popular in Georgian and Mediterranean architecture, also utilize the creative cycle: Metal nurtures water. The element to avoid is earth, so don't use the entry for storage or leaving things; that's why there are closets. Earth objects like shelves, low tables, and good rugs don't feel right or work in this space anyway. Here's an old nostrum that makes sense in the light of water energy: An unusual, mysterious object partly hidden in the entry will bring unusual visitors (sympathetic magic at work). We hope it's not the FBI.

The Living Room. This is the main social room of the home, and in many cases it's called the family room or den. It's important, again, that function come first. A case in point: A midwestern family used a formal, pristine, overdecorated living room once a year, when they put up a Christmas tree—guests would come in, gawk, then go to the family room to socialize. After a consultation, they made the living room into a library, which solved their major clutter issue and also made the house more functional. So for many of us this family room is where we really live, as in talk, watch TV/DVDs, play music, entertain, or just lay around like a pride of lions after a wildebeest feast. The home theater/multimedia center location is the "DGA"—dead giveaway. This room, because it is multifunctional, partakes of more than one element, usually wood if the space is used for creative or work activities, fire if for study and thought, metal if for certain kinds of entertainment (like enjoying music), and especially water if it's a social center or used for communication. A hearth and fireplace are often the heart of the room. Since this space is where guests are entertained, the blessing/curse of "decoration" and "style" rears its dragon head here more than in any other room (although dining rooms can come close). A few guidelines will be helpful: The more functions that the room supports the more the need for simplicity and a pared-down essentialism; elements work better together when they're relatively pure and plain. And the more people who use the room, the less it can reflect one individual sensibility, stylistically or practically. Also, the more the room is used the greater and faster it will change, as life energies are always evolving; don't resist but assist. Daughter off to college? Lose the Xbox. More hungry regular visitors? Add a serving trolley or buffet table. And so on.

The Kitchen. The heart of any kitchen is the stove, which is of course affiliated with fire, as is the kitchen proper, where the transformations (many of them chemical) required by food preparation take place. Most modern kitchen designs use a combination of wood and metal elements, which feed and stimulate fire, respectively. Yet too much metal in a kitchen, besides looking industrial, overemphasizes restraint and will make the kitchen feel uncreative and uninspired. We shouldn't overdo the earth element here, either, as it can deplete fire; in earlier centuries, storage functions, as found in pantries, root cellars, larders, creameries, and so forth, all earth-affiliated spaces, were kept separate from the kitchen proper (which also helped retard spoilage from the kitchen's heat). Moreover, storage functions shouldn't compromise our work space and get in the way of cooking. The French, expert in such things, call *mis-en-place* the art of getting set up to cook, so that a chef has all necessary tools and ingredients ready to go at his or her fingertips when a certain dish must be made; they realized that the two functions can be separated spatially and often temporally. Last, confine the water element, which restrains fire, to the sink or to be hidden in the dishwasher. Ideally, washing is done far away from the stove—a placement not going to happen in today's studio-sized kitchenettes. Also watch out for glass near the stove—a window over the stove is just not smart (vapor, spatters, dirt, distraction, and so on). Putting this all together, since food preparation is so fundamental a human activity, the kitchen should receive as much design care and expense as anywhere else in the house, ergonomically, energetically, environmentally, and so on. As the nineteenth-century gastronome Brillat-Savarin once said, "Show me how a person selects his food, prepares it, eats it, and digests it, and I'll tell you everything about him."

Dining Area. In many homes, people eat right next to their kitchen or in an adjacent dinette, even when they have a dining area, which may seem like it saves time and trouble (so does eating out of the pot) but diminishes the spiritual side of eating. The abundance of relatively cheap food and the ease and speed of many preparations have spoiled us. Eating is a sacred act, a gift from Heaven through the bounty of the Earth, which should never be taken for granted. The sweat and toil of thousands of generations of ancestors have brought billions of us some degree of abundance. The meal is the one moment when the family is sure to gather together and also the heart of holy-day (holiday) activities. The Last Supper and Mass/Communion (coming into union) distinguish Christianity; Passover is also significant in Judaism. So even in smaller apartments or homes without a real dining room, make the eating area as special a space as possible, whether through extraordinary tablecloths, flatware, and china, or through unique decorations on and around the table. When we eat, "the boss" is always coming to dinner. In recent times, the Slow Food movement has been trying to bring back some of the ritual importance of meals. Because of the highly desirable inclusiveness of sharing food, the best dining rooms balance all the elements, even when there's a clearly defined design style that may favor one pattern over another. This balance is well symbolized by the chafing dish, candelabra, or vase of red or pink flowers placed in the center of the dining table, centering the fire element; the flatware adds metal; the dishes earth; the glassware water; and the table wood. Sometimes a single artifact can combine all five: The Russian samovar features a rounded container (metal) holding a liquid (water) over a fire on a stand (wood) that holds the ash (earth). In many Italian dining rooms, ornately sculptural, altarlike espresso machines dramatically symbolize this universal alchemy. A really successful dining area should do so as well.

The Bathroom. In traditional feng shui, meaning in premodern China, this room was considered noxious for obvious reasons. Nowadays, with indoor plumbing—flowing instead of stagnant water—as well as the rise of a huge body-care industry, the bathroom has become for many people a refuge and mini-spa. This is a healthy trend, but it also means that earth and water, namely, bodily health, storage, cleaning, and bathing, must be harmonized. This is most easily done by adding metal, and circular mirrors, round tables, glass globes, and curved bowls have been popular and successful, so much so that, energetically speaking, the bathroom is the most balanced space in many homes. This can have amusing and unintended consequences, as when household members use it for reading and as a general refuge. There's nothing wrong with that; indeed, an even stronger balance is achieved by adding wood and fire, such as in a traditional Asian or European bathhouse, but in a private home it requires considerable space and expense. Who wouldn't want a sauna in their bathroom? The bath is often where we are closest to our bodies, and it deserves the positive attention that in older cultures was demonstrated by their luxurious, lavish bathhouses, virtual temples to our earthly form. Even today, from Japan to Russia to Morocco, public bathing is a lengthy, relaxing, usually social activity that may yet catch on in the United States.

The Bedroom. One generally expects this room to be filled with quiet and repose, an oasis of rejuvenation and comfort. The earth element, the most tranquil, usually dominates, in the form of beds, futons, low tables, dressers, and furniture for clothes storage. Because fire supports earth, many bedroom designs promote the fire element, from pointed finials on bed canopies, highboys, and headboards, to decorative hats, masks, and the use of the color red. Fire energies also can promote Eros effectively. Be careful that the wood element, which restrains earth, isn't too strong in this room, for it could leave the occupants more tired than they were before entering. This explains why we hardly ever see a strongly green-colored bedroom; when we do find one in a well-designed home, it has many round objects or metal pieces, as metal restrains wood. Nurseries, on the other hand, are more sympathetic to the wood element. There the vigorous growth and development of children is as high a priority as rest and recuperation.

Miscellaneous Rooms. Studios often affiliate with the wood element, because of the premium set on creative growth and the making of new forms. Libraries are sometimes used for thinking and inspiration, connected with fire, although more often than not they are storage areas (for books, tapes, discs, and so on) and remain connected to earth. Conservatories, greenhouses, and porches filled with plants naturally align with wood. Recreation centers and gyms, because they're concerned with health and physical exercise, affiliate with both the earth element and, depending on how much competition occurs there, the fire element. On the other hand, game rooms, billiard rooms, and computer rooms, where judgment and discrimination rule, affiliate with metal. Playrooms, social areas, and even some sacred spaces evoke water, whereas many ritual and religious spaces, such as chapels, meditation rooms, and worship areas usually resonate with fire.

The Office. For those of us managing some kind of business, Appendix II summarizes the five phases of change in the business cycle; here we'll consider only the elemental basics of offices. Many offices of course concern themselves with money and financial matters, and they associate with metal through emphasis on discrimination, accounting, following rules, organizing beautifully, and balancing the books. But that's not the whole story; these metal functions are only part of most businesses; other departments, divisions, subsections, or whole companies will affiliate otherwise. Many executive functions, such as administration (creating structure) and project initiation, as well as business growth and expansion, evoke wood. Inspiring leadership, market insight, and even company charisma depend on elemental fire. Many firms focus on preservation, continuity, and running a stable bureaucracy, all earth functions; earth also governs storing or maintaining goods, services, and even individuals, exemplified by personnel departments. Then there's an entire class of water-related business functions that focus on communications, transportation, and dispersing ideas, people, or materials: Advertising, shipping, and publishing are common examples. The petroleum industry ("Big Oil") often shows many of the negative aspects of a strongly water-related business: secrecy, defensiveness, ruthlessness, and megalomania. So depending on what the employee—and the company—actually does in any given cubicle, floor, office or plant, any of the Five Elements may dominate the environment.

Moving Day and How Not to Go Nuts

One of the most important activities that we'll ever do in our home or office is to leave it for a new one. Earlier it was suggested that moving should be a positive event. Let's go further: Many people don't move enough because of their fears. What's more, increasing numbers of us are no longer rooted to one village, one city, one language, or one nationality. There's an increasingly planetary consciousness of where home lies and a growing interest in dwelling on different parts of the globe. And that means dwelling in the sense of living fully in, with, and from a particular place, not "living at" some address, where life is like e-mail sent to Singapore while stopping in New York on a trip to Sao Paulo. Yet even if we move only a few times in life, there are energetic strategies to help moving day, which psychologists have found to be one of the most traumatic times in many people's lives, become a more enriching experience.

We should ask ourselves why moving is so traumatic. Birth, graduation, marriage, and passing are all traumatic in their own ways, but over time cultures have evolved rituals to appreciate and sanctify life's major transitions, connecting them with the larger forces in the cosmos. For most of history, we have stayed rooted to the farm, village, or town in which we were born, so the sanctification of moving never much evolved. So what's needed on moving day is a ritual approach to tie the fuss, trouble, and headache to the coming excitement of positive change and growth. The following practice is based on East Asian customs, but it brings together all Five Elements and can be adapted to our different spiritual traditions.

Three days before the move, take a red silk handkerchief or red piece of cloth (silk is preferable for the occasion) and sit with it in some kind of meditation for at least several minutes. Recall everything that you can possibly remember of any significance that happened to you or that you did in that space, neither clinging to the memory nor deliberately pushing it away. Just observe. Sleep that night with the red silk under your pillow. Two days before the move, and then again one day before, repeat the meditation, and if it's faster or slower, more or less detailed, it doesn't matter. Keep the silk under your pillow when not used in the meditation. On moving day, when it's time for you to leave the space for the last time, spread the red silk over the threshold and depart while imagining, speaking, or chanting an appropriate prayer or incantation. Buddhists may say *"Gate, gate, paragate"* or "Om mani padme hum"; Jews may recite parts of the Kaddish; Christians could recite the Lord's Prayer; and agnostics could pick favorite musical lyrics or poetry. One salesman left his office reciting the words to Elton John's "Goodbye Yellow Brick Road." When you're finished, on the other side of the threshold, pick up the silk, fold it, and take it to the new space. In moving it's inevitable that something we value will be damaged or broken. Wrap the damaged item in the silk and bury it (if burial is not convenient, as in the middle of a large city, ceremoniously burn the item and scatter the ashes outside the new threshold) with at least a few friends and family present. Be mindful, and then express it through a few remarks to the assembled, that an old way of life is dead. Then, finally, have a celebratory feast. You'll feel deeply released from the old space and ready to fully inhabit the new. If—praise Heaven—nothing is damaged in moving, or you can't unpack immediately, or you're leaving all the furnishings behind, as in from a hotel room or a company-owned workspace, pick something distinctive from that place, like a pebble, a pencil, or a photo, and use that instead.

Walking the Walk

Field trip, hooray! Our understanding of the Five Elements has grown deeper, so we can try a more involved exercise. Choose a site that you've never seen before or perhaps noticed only at a glance. It could be down the road or a short drive away, or maybe worked into a visit to another locale; it could be a business, commercial space, or public area. If you wish to visit a home, it should be one open to the public, because any work in a private area should be done at the owner's request, and such work is not a beginner's exercise. Because there are so many educational, tourist, and historical sites across the country, finding such a home will not be a hardship and will be bound to be fascinating on many levels. Make sure there will be at least a handful of main rooms to study. Bring the notebook and note all impressions of activities, all uses and configurations of materials, all affiliations with the elements, and all energy in general. As the elements normally indicate different kinds of change, watch their interplay and how they affect the ch'i. Often more than one visit is necessary, as environments are always changing, even if the changes are slow and subtle. A first visit, for example, to a furniture maker's factory was only partially useful (but still quite marvelous) because none of the workers were there. While impressions of wood and earth dominated that trip, when actual fabrication was in high gear, metal and fire objects and activities came much more to the fore. Don't try to synthesize very much while taking in the space, for many things will pop into the mind after the visit—so keep the notebook handy the following day. If associations strike you at any time, just write them down, neglecting nothing that comes to mind. Before leaving, review what's written and feel whether there's anything calling to be seen again before leaving the site.

Another fun and insightful exercise is to grab the notebook and sketch, doodle, or plan an ideal dream house/vacation house/office/apartment/factory. Forget expense and practicality; just reflect the heart's wishes and indulge the imagination, denying no serious impulse. If you dream of a pool in your house, then with all that water, where should it be and how should it look? How can it be most harmoniously integrated into the rest of the place? Very few of us have not imagined a dream building at some point, but have we analyzed its

elemental connections? This can be quite insightful in terms of our own type and learning about ourselves.

> *A building is like a human; an architect has the*
> *opportunity of creating life. The way the knuckles*
> *and joints come together make each hand interesting*
> *and beautiful. In a building these details should*
> *not be put in a mitten and hidden. Space is*
> *architectural when the evidence of how it is*
> *made is seen and comprehended.*
>
> —LOUIS KAHN, TWENTIETH-CENTURY ARCHITECT [1]

CHAPTER EIGHT

For More Experienced Students—Keeping the Path Fresh

 t's common in feng shui work to get caught up in parsing elemental affiliations, searching for subtle changes in energy, and dwelling on swings from Yin to Yang to the point where a sense of the overall path is lost. Tao doesn't rent a billboard and grandly announce that we must pause, stop everything, and intuit our bearings. Rather, in a quiet moment the impression will steal upon us that we're moving through a bunch of trees but we don't know the forest. So this last chapter is a way of rounding the circle, again, by way of getting back to that ineffable something that takes the work to a whole different level—and finding the nose

right in front of our face once more. To do that, we have to shake things up and go against the grain a bit. Sure, it's good to know the ideas; it's even better to put them wisely and creatively into practice. Positive changes will often ensue, and occasionally not. But the danger, mentioned in the previous chapter in relation to business, is that with growth and success we'll desire to hold on to what we've got and resist further change (wood-fire-earth again). We'll want to keep cashing in on what worked yesterday and set up strict rules and regulations for how we practice (metal). But then let's remember to let go of them, dissolve them (water)! Try to see beyond all dogma and orthodoxy. And in turn this dissolution is another stage to pass through. As water feeds wood, new growth will appear again.

The Not-Doing of Environmental Adjustment

The master sculptor doesn't carve.

—Tao Te Ching, Verse 28

Lao Tsu's words recall Michelangelo's comment that he didn't carve marble; he revealed and released a form that he perceived was already inside the stone. We could say he was finely attuned to the ch'i in marble. This is a great attitude to take in adjusting our spaces. Nothing should appear forced or out of place; all the parts should feel and look to us like they belong there together, and, at that moment, always have been. Moreover, adjustments work more efficaciously when they don't call attention to themselves; for one, they won't bring in the distraction of other people's unrelated opinions and comments. There's the example of a family's comfy, colonial era–inspired living room jarred one weekend by a bright red and gold octagonal Chinese mirror in the southeast corner.

> "I feng shui'ed it myself," Dad said proudly, "so we'll have more money."
>
> Mom asked, "Where did you get that idea?"
>
> "The newspaper—daily feng shui tips or something like that."
>
> "Well, the mirror maker certainly has more money now."

(And talk about mechanically following somebody else's rule.) So Mom talked Dad into replacing the mirror with an interesting painting related to their locale that also enhanced the room rather than turning part of it into a Hong Kong bordello. The family is doing just fine financially, too. In another example, a businesswoman complained that her boss made repeated snide remarks about a wind chime she had hung over her desk. "I feel like suing him for weakening the ch'i," she fumed. Rather than get into hot water, when she merely wanted to enhance her performance she wisely tried something else, hanging at the entrance to her office a lively photo of a company outing at an amusement park. Her boss and coworkers loved the fun picture, and it also sent the message that she cared about the firm and its priorities. In the extreme case, when there is no possibility of changing a room at all, for one reason or another (it's rented, no funds, a historic preservation trust, and so on), we can use our imaginations to actively change the feeling and the perception of the space whenever we're in it. One businessman often paused in his office to hear an invisible seashore nearby. It just takes strong intention and memory.

We can take this subtle, Taoist approach of letting

things be to a further degree and explore the blending of new and old, used and pristine. Rooms, including offices, that look "perfect," meaning everything is clean, new, shiny, and in place, are at an extreme Yang moment. They will inevitably change toward Yin like the ocean's tides. It will make life easier and more rewarding to not fight this tide too hard; while cleanliness will almost always improve the ch'i, it can be taken to an unproductive extreme. For example, a craftsman who vacuums his studio every morning, whether it has picked up a speck of dust or not, could be catching up on reading, messages, or returning calls. While some folks find rituals such as scrubbing already spotless floors calming, let's ask whether the time and energy thus spent have better uses. Families with young children know that you can do little more than conduct rear-guard action against spills, breakage, and mess. Furniture will show nicks and gouges; crockery will chip; and carpets will fade and show wear spots. At the same time, new pieces are entering the household in the continual flux of life itself. There's no point in trying to dictate, as opposed to guide, this natural evolution. There's the added bonus that the more things wear down the easier it will be to replace or eliminate them.

As football Coach Jimmy Johnson said when he was at the helm of the Miami Dolphins, "It's a heck of a lot easier to make a lousy team great than to make a good team great." (This leads to a useful question for any business: How do we overcome the good as the enemy of the great, or how far should we push for continual improvements?) Again and again, with fresh eyes, we ask ourselves what things naturally fit, right here, right now? Thus we can paraphrase Lao Tsu and say that the best designer doesn't design. Something else Lao Tsu also wrote applies here: "Be persevering, not arrogant. Attain your ends, but not with force. To force things to grow before their time, which is against Tao, will only cause their decline" (*Tao Te Ching*, Verse 30).

Don't Always Avoid a Void—Using Dynamic Emptiness

In order for something of quality to take place, an empty space needs to be created. An empty space makes it possible for a new phenomenon to come to life, for anything that touches on content, meaning, expression, language, and music can only exist if the experience is fresh and new.

—PETER BROOK, THEATER DIRECTOR

Earlier we saw that in improving the energy of a space, instead of actively adding something, we often subtract. Experiment with clearing away and emptying a part of a room; create a void. Our model is Taoist meditation, a huge subject by itself (see the bibliography for recommended books), which strongly emphasizes the regular clearing/emptying of the mind-body continuum. We saw the value of this before visiting a site: Relax the body, calm the heart, quiet the mind. There is certainly an analogous need in just about every building and room for an area that's quiet and calming. This is not the same as a "dead space" that feels like it needs something—just the opposite: This space wants to be left empty. But we must be aware of Tao enough so that we continually perceive that void as dynamic and active, as creating something new. This adjustment is particularly helpful if life seems filled with too much change and agitation.

Most rooms, with the exception of dining and

sleeping areas and small offices, deliberately keep a center area open for good circulation; this doesn't count. We need to experiment with emptying another spot of everything or just about everything. Any objects left will then gain significant symbolic value, so choose the area very mindfully, making maximum use of your intuition. Along that line, make a mental commitment to pay attention to this area and feel/imagine what it does to you and to the room. How do you feel physically and emotionally when you spend time in this sector? See if you're more connected between your inner vision and outer activities. If the void is in an office, has business changed, and how? Are you recognized more,

sent on trips, complete tasks sooner, or work better with partners? There is precious information to be learned, including which elements have been supported. And remember, this is a dynamic situation; at some point the void will *tell us* what needs to be added there, if anything, and we need to then contemplate the meaning of that message. An added, marvelous bonus is that we'll strongly appreciate the creative power of emptiness, of spatial and material silence. It can be golden.

The Taoist acceptance of change, including growth and decay, supports the growing school of environmentally conscious design that uses recyclable materials that need never land in a landfill. These even include appliances and furniture, not just bottles, papers, and cans. Recycling invokes the circle of transformations, such as the Five Elements themselves, and our culture needs to remember that cycles, like the circle of life itself, are sacred. Why not view the integration of our rooms into the world at large, including recycling, as a sacred duty? It's impossible for any building not be connected to the Earth and prosper, as the failure of the Biosphere project showed succinctly.

Embracing Age and
Wabi-sabi Design

We can go even further than "letting things be" and actively insert environmental elements that show off, even revel in, their age, weathering, wear-and-tear, and even decay. It's a form of environmental meditation, among other things, and it requires a more evolved sense of time and life's cycles. In Japan this style is called Wabi-sabi, and it has a deeply spiritual character, appreciative of impermanence, chance, and quiet. This aesthetic is also an alternative to extensive recycling; here we just keep using worn and organically aging materials—materials that are not deliberately antique—until they fail. Although it's easy to mock those trendy "shabby-chic" rooms as a mere reaction against the always-new-and-improved paradigm, Wabi-sabi searches for truth in imperfection with a Zenlike depth and detachment. For some people, the best environment is like the renowned Stilton cheese: It needs a little spoilage. This approach takes extreme intention, restraint, and detachment; otherwise the living room meant to look like a Zen garden can more closely resemble a junkyard. But when it works, the impact, especially on a spiritual level, is stunning. Rust on metal siding is beautiful. Old jugs and weathered benches become visual poetry. As I've mentioned earlier, life takes on a more vital awareness of itself when decay and death are naturally present. And in a culture filled with rampant ageism and excessive consumerism, Wabi-sabi is profoundly fresh and refreshing. What's more, it's deeply in tune with the "green building" movement and the creation of less environmentally harmful and disruptive structures—and finding a whole new aesthetic in the process.[1] Further information on this fascinating school can be found in the bibliography. Whether it becomes understood and cultivated in the United States, not merely hip or "flavor of the month," will say something about the evolution of our own goals, including our ideas of health and success. The spiritual cast of the Wabi-sabi philosophy and its deeply Taoist underpinnings are strikingly captured in T. S. Eliot's poem "East Coker" from his *Four Quartets*:

> In my beginning is my end. In succession
> Houses rise and fall, crumble, are extended,

Are removed, destroyed, restored, or in their place
Is an open field, or a factory, or a by-pass.
Old stone to new building, old timber to new fires,
Old fire to new ashes, and ashes to the earth
Which is already flesh, fur and feces,
Bone of man and beast, cornstalk and leaf.

In Conclusion, Words of Encouragement from a Few Masters

Once you begin working in depth with feng shui, environmental energies, and the like, you may feel exhilarated, flush with your fresh store of knowledge and anticipating some great insight, achievement, or success. Off you go on your project, and who needs a conclusion, of all things? Then, inevitably, comes a letdown, often stemming from a question of what to do next and a fear that what has been done thus far is misguided. We've all been there before, in one form or another, because it's part of a universal pattern. This very Yin moment is just the time to try to receive some kind of feeling or intuition of Tao. So don't fight any uncertain, hesitant, or negative feelings; instead, really experience them and live them, for the seeds of the next Yang phase—whether it's a new insight, discovery, activity, something hot and bright—lie within this cold and dark moment. The eminent twentieth-century architect Alvar Aalto described this process wonderfully:

> When I personally have some architectural problem to solve, I am constantly . . . faced with an obstacle difficult to surmount, a kind of "three in the morning feeling." The reason seems to be the complicated, heavy burden represented by the fact that architectural planning operates with innumerable elements, which often conflict. Social, human, economic, and technical demands combined with psychological questions affecting both the individual and the group, together with movements of human masses and individuals, and internal frictions all form a complex tangle which cannot be unraveled in a rational or mechanical way. The immense number of different demands and component problems constitute a barrier from behind which

it is difficult for the basic idea to emerge . . . I forget the entire mass of problems for a while, after the atmosphere of the job and the innumerable difficult requirements have sunk into my subconscious. Then I move on to a method of working which is very much like abstract art. I just draw by instinct, not architectural synthesis, but what are sometimes childlike compositions, and in this way, on this abstract basis, the main idea gradually takes shape, a kind of universal substance which helps me to bring innumerable contradictory component problems into harmony.[2]

We'd be hard-pressed to find a better description of the Taoist approach. And this approach has been the goal of what we've read here: not just a way of improving our outer environment but also our inner world and all, inside and out, that connects to it. A more successful home is just *our real home;* a more successful job or business is just *our real work,* which means a sincere, adventurous, exciting search for what is true and good. That will be beautiful.

Some of us will want to go further in some of the

directions suggested above, continuing to move along paths that have been barely introduced or suggested. Sources are listed below for further explorations of ch'i building such as t'ai ch'i and ch'i kung; more extended Taoist meditation exercises and health practices, often using the Five Elements; and further studies of architecture, philosophy, history, and other goodies touched on so far. Enjoy, and remember, too, that the path is as much the goal, and the sleep and the forgetting are as much of life as the planning and the building. Lao Tsu, appropriately, challenges us to find success, that is, to live every moment within our fullest, most whole self— and that challenge is where we shall end, for now:

> Cut from the cloth of both flesh and spirit, can one harmonious garment of Tao clothe your being? Charged with ch'i, bursting with vital energy, can you be as soft and supple as a baby? Cleansed of all superfluities, can you mirror the deepest truth of the world? Could you care for the people and govern the country yet retain a beginner's mind? Could you withstand a storm in Heaven and tumult on Earth like a mother bird on

her nest? As your brilliance penetrates to the edge of the Universe, could you still follow the way of non-action? Then go create without taking credit, nurture without demanding results, lead without taking control, and show the profound virtue of Tao! (*Tao Te Ching*, Verse 10).

Learning Activities

T. S. Eliot also wrote, "In the end is my beginning." The end of the book, it is hoped, is the beginning of a sincere and successful practice of feng shui. What exactly will happen? Who knows, but here's a great meditation that focuses on transformation: Say the local newspaper in the year 2020 (online, handheld digital, or beyond) writes about your life with emphasis on feng shui projects. Imagine this article in as much detail as possible, and throw in all the relevant life material—family situation, business, personal success, various achievements, and so on. The point is to imagine a progress report on life with feng shui, *as we would* like it to be. Be as realistic, reasonable, and as hopeful as possible. Balance where the imagination wants to pull you with what has already happened. If you're unsettled deep down somewhere, that's good; all too rarely do we ask ourselves big-picture questions about what we are really doing with our lives. Imagine how feng shui has helped. Then, after several days, look at your article and ask: How do we get there from here? Make some kind of plan, or group of plans given life's contingencies, to move your trip along, using the practices we've seen so far. Or create new ones! The key is to see yourself as you are now, and using ch'i cultivation and element work, realize how your state of being right at this very moment is the only bridge you can build to your best possible future. As Lao Tsu wrote:

> Let people take death seriously and not live other than in the here and now. Let people return to simple, true words; relish their food; beautify their clothes; create harmony in their homes and find joy in everyday life (*Tao Te Ching*, Verse 80).

APPENDICES

Appendix I. Relating the Five Elements to Traditional Design Styles

Wood:

Wood activities and attitudes focus on expansion and administration and so dominate many business offices, regardless of outer appearance. Sites dedicated to research, discovery, and creative work also generate wood energy. Wood styles give an impression of growth and linearity, and can range from clean to quite elaborate, with a "forest" of detail. Wood element rooms are a good place to stimulate joy, laughter, and talk (fire activities): Elizabethan, Jacobean, French Renaissance (Louis XIII), Louis Quatorze (Louis XIV), Restoration (Stuart), and then Neoclassic-influenced styles such as Louis Seize (Louis XVI), Sheraton, Greek Revival, and, later,

Prairie (Stickley is an example). Wood colors include greens, like hunt or Kelly, and also violets and purples.

Fire:

Sharp, pointed styles are rare in homes, usually because folks go to churches, temples, or schools for inspiration and other fire-related, transformational activities. There's also the practical consideration of using these shapes when there are kids and seniors around. Fire styles include Gothic Revival and Gothic-inspired Arts-and-Crafts as well as occasional modern and postmodern designs. (Note that Gothic Revival was a style of the Victorian era, when children were not allowed in a home's principal rooms.) Many Asian carpets have a fiery quality and can add energy to otherwise quiet spaces. Fire color schemes center on reds, red-oranges, and pinks.

Earth:

Earth activities include preservation, storage, and comfort seeking. Earth interiors and styles are thus common, including solid, blocky, or low designs, and quite diverse, such as Spanish Colonial (not the earlier Spanish Renaissance, which was more wood- and fire-inspired), the Dutch-influenced William and Mary, Frontier and Shaker, Craftsman-period

Arts-and-Crafts, such as William Morris as well as Art Deco, North African, International Style, and Machine Modern. Traditional Japanese interiors primarily evoke the earth element with secondary wood. Many earth rooms are calm and homey. Earth colors tend to oranges, yellows, and browns.

Metal:

Finance, law, and curating exemplify metal activities, where discrimination and judgment are paramount. Metal styles often feature arches and circles, especially in chairs and tables: Italianate, and its Victorian imitators, Italian Renaissance, Queen Anne, English Adam, some American rustic and colonial, First Empire, Scandinavian Modern (like Eero Saarinen), some Mediterranean Modern as well as many Islamic styles, like Turkish—as seen in ottomans. Many of these rooms feel formal or even elegant, often in an impersonal way. Metal-affiliated colors are in the white-to-gray range; some popular colors, like beige, sit on the fence between earth and metal.

Water:

This diverse element, symbolized by rushing streams as well as great oceans, relates to communication, commingling, and contemplation. Water styles feature serpentine or irregular shapes, like Rococo and its offshoots, including Louis Quinze (Louis XV); Late Georgian, as in Thomas Chippendale; Regency; and, later, Art Nouveau (works by Louis Comfort Tiffany and Antoni Gaudí are iconic examples) as well as some South Asian and East Asian designs. Rooms completed in these styles often feel quite artistic, others frothy. The blue range of the color wheel affiliates with water, naturally, including ultramarine blue as well as black.

Appendix II. Relating the Five Elements to Phases of the Business Cycle

Many business models depict firms or commercial enterprises as machines, impervious to many external conditions and locked into a limited number of fixed responses to change. An organic entity, such as a garden or pond, is much more accurate as a model. This model emphasizes interrelatedness, mutual dependency, contingency, and consensual, evolving harmony. (Of course, more evolved organizations show degrees of consciousness that transcend any model, but we're not there yet.) While the whole is greater than the sum of its parts, the health of the whole depends on the health of all the parts. An organic model shows how patterns of change unfold naturally and where parts needing nurturing or restraint can be found. Recall the Five Element cycle, wood-fire-earth-metal-water, which symbolizes the progression, in less general terms, from growth to transformation to preservation to discrimination to dissolution and back to growth. Each element has an effect on each of the four others, encouraging or discouraging, and this interconnectedness is part of what makes the model organic. Any business can be explored in light of its components or functions based on the Five Elements. The following summary emphasizes questions related to each element; if your answer indicates less than optimal functioning, let's use what we've learned earlier to adjust that element.

Water functions:

Among other things, the water element governs the challenging aspects of our work, such as pitfalls, dangers, and potential problems. What are they, and are we over- or under reacting to them? How are we prepared for slowdowns and other cold periods? Other water issues involve people as a mass, like a reservoir or lake: What is the labor force like, and how are the people working with us? Is hard work rewarded and is it rewarding? What are relations with our customers like? Let's not forget communication inside and outside the firm, including public relations and advertising, all water-connected: Are we getting the right message to the right people at the right time? Water also symbolizes the unknown: Are there hidden opportunities afoot? Also, what are the quirks, oddities, and funny things about our business? Water also connects to the completion of things, as endings also prepare the way for new beginnings. Does the firm get stuck in the mud, so to speak, right when it needs to move? As the sage of the New York Yankees, Yogi Berra, once said, "When you come to a fork in the road, take it."

Wood-related activities:

Are projects being started in a positive way? What are the opportunities available to the business? What needs to be made new? How does the company (or how do we) handle initiative? Growth is a key issue for many businesses; is it over- or underemphasized, and, in any case, is it solid and steady or weak and intermittent? Do administrative tasks and duties get done promptly, thoroughly, and energetically? Is the company structured in the most productive way, and do the various chains of command work in a good way? Wood also affiliates with travel, which is crucial to certain businesses; we need to ask if more or less is needed, if it's helping the firm, and if different kinds of travel may be required. What is the company's philosophy, and is it working well? Is it broad-minded and expansive enough? Does the company support education, within and without? Finally, is planning for growth and change taken seriously? As Henry Ford once said, "Before everything else, getting ready is the secret of success."

Fire:

What is the boss or the company leadership like? Is authority respected? Is the firm under control? Is it creative or inspiring enough? Are the company's products inspiring or inspired; do they show something special, beyond the same-old, same-old? Is the work creative enough, or is it stuck in stultifying routine? What is at the heart of the business or what is its soul? Is there enough energy to get done what has to be done, let alone explore new avenues of work? Is there enough intensity in the work? Does the company have enough benefactors? How does the company appear to the public? Is its reputation sterling or tarnished? Does the firm get the recognition it deserves? How does the company handle conflict? Is it capable, if necessary, of waging and winning a business war? Here's an apt quotation from the journalist Dorothy Thompson on this subject: "Peace is not the absence of conflict, but the presence of creative alternatives for responding to conflict."

Earth:

What are the resource levels of the business? Is there a cushion to the cash flow, adequate financing, capital, assets, and inventory for a rainy day? Is there reasonably enough profit to build up reserves? Is the firm (and are we as workers) obsessed, prudent, or careless with money and other resources? Is there enough space (of all types) and enough storage for the work to proceed comfortably? Is there a sense of family togetherness, or belonging, within the company? Do the employees feel at home? Is there support for them, through benefits, insurance, savings, and so on (the safety net)? How does the firm take care of its people? Are there enough breaks, vacations, down time, and other forms of R&R for the business to regenerate and stay healthy? Are there quiet moments or periods of reflection available? Is there a sense of continuity, tradition, and value in the work? More important than any external judgment of intelligence, a company's (or a person's) real IQ should mean its level of inner quiet. When inner quiet is real, no outer disaster, no matter how severe, can destroy the essential quality of the organism.

Metal:

Are money and other forms of valuables or currency, including intellectual currency such as research, handled with intelligence and discrimination? Is the workforce (or are we) knowledgeable and skilled about the business? Does the firm encourage R&D—research and development—to continually refine and improve the work or the products? Does the firm keep good records and cultivate knowledge? Is the work done efficiently, with all *t*'s crossed and *i*'s dotted? Are the company's rules clear, the regulations fair, and are the workers clear as to their responsibilities and obligations? We also need to watch out for too much of a metal influence—are things done too much by the book? Are rules and regulations too picayune, petty, and unproductive? On the other hand, are relations among the customers, employees, labor, management, and so on, harmonious and principled? When (not if) things get out of line, are problems handled with justice and equanimity? Are superfluities, and even unneeded workers, sent away cleanly and fairly? Is there an overall aesthetic level to the work, an appreciation of beauty and proportion?

NOTES

Introduction

1. The so-called green movement to limit global warming and preserve the natural environment is generally in close accord with feng shui principles. Recycling obviously enhances environmental energetics. Next, take wasted energy, which of course creates bad ch'i. The average American family spends about $1,500 on energy costs per year and, according to the Rocky Mountain Institute, can reduce those costs 10 to 90 percent. Some of these reductions take an initial investment, like purchasing insulation; upgrading thermostats, heaters, faucets, and showerheads; buying energy-efficient appliances and lightbulbs; and weatherizing windows and doors. But eventually they pay for themselves many times over. And look what we can do to save lots of money with no up-front investment: Turn down the water heater thermostat to 120 degrees Fahrenheit; turn off lights and close heating units in unused rooms; don't waste water; lower thermostats; repair water and air leaks; and clean the refrigerator's coils. And that's just a start!

Notes

Chapter One: Taoism and the Roots of Feng Shui

1. The translations of the *Tao Te Ching* are the author's, unless otherwise noted. The author is grateful for the excellent ideogram analysis provided by Jonathan Star in his definitive edition.

Chapter Two: Improving Ch'i and Increasing Life Energy

1. Nili Portugali, "A Holistic Approach to Architecture and Its Implementation in the Physical and Cultural Context of the Place." http://www.umbau-verlag.com/Essays/NiliPortugali.html.

2. See note 2 to Chapter 4.

Chapter Four: The Vital Energy of the Home and Business Environments

1. Natural and recycled materials used by contemporary architects and builders include specially compressed hay bales, bricks made of recycled products such as glass and fiber, and bricks made of metal cages that hold stone, gravel, and rock. Rather than seeing these elements as design liabilities compared with traditional stone, brick, and wood, many innovative architects and builders have discovered that they have marvelous insulation, durability, texture, and other mechanical and aesthetic properties. The Dominus Winery in Napa, California, for example, designed by the Swiss architects Herzog and de Meuron, uses wire-mesh walls filled with stones to create a warehouselike shed and office block with carefully proportioned planes and openings. The effect of the intense Napa sun filtered through the loose rock is amazing. The architects write,

"For light filters through the masses, forming an ever-changing weave which depends on atmospheric conditions and the shapes of the stones: the effect is something entirely new, rather like a fascinating brise-soleil, repeated in the glass in the office area. On the other hand, the 'cuts' through which vehicles gain access into the massive bulk of the construction permit it to connect up with the restful hilly landscape behind it." For this kind of ingenuity, the architects were awarded the profession's highest award, the Pritzker Prize.

2. The environmental history of New Orleans, one of the most historically and culturally important cities in America, shows dramatic highs and lows: While the shotgun house and French Quarter townhouse show respectful accommodation to the local environment, the bad feng shui engendered by vast, thoughtless engineering "marvels" may end up literally sinking the city. A partial, sad list: Straight shipping channels allow ocean ch'i to head right to the city—Hurricane Katrina's storm surge went right into the port area; damming of the Mississippi has prevented silt from nourishing and regenerating barrier islands to the south of the city, thus destroying the natural line of defense against storm surges. Without a natural outflow of silt, it goes to the river bottom and raises the river, and levees must be built ever higher, increasing the danger of flooding; and the massive draining of swamps around the city for overdevelopment has placed large residential areas under the threat of continued flooding as well as deprived the area of natural drains and buffers for flood waters.

*Chapter Five: Enriching Home and Business Sites
with the Five Elements*

1. Check out the regal *and* beautiful Castle Howard in Britain for how this effect may have looked, albeit on a smaller scale.

Chapter Six: Creating Good Energy Inside Home and Office

1. Rudolf Schindler, "Care of the Body," *Los Angeles Times*, March 14, 1926.

Chapter Seven: The Five Elements and Indoor Patterns of Change

1. Quoted from Heinz Ronner, with Sharad Jhaveri and Alessandro Vasella, *Louis I. Kahn: Complete Works 1935–74* (Boulder, CO: Westview, 1977), p. 116.

Chapter Eight: For More Experienced Students—Keeping the Path Fresh

1. Given that human civilization appeared in riverside locations with important seasonal flood cycles—the Nile, the Tigris-Euphrates (in Mesopotamia, renamed Iraq by the British in 1920, from an Arabic word meaning "shore"), the Indus, and the Yellow River—we might have hoped that productive, harmonious cooperation with river ecology would have evolved. Fat chance; even the Chinese, midwives to classic Taoism, began building levees and silting up the Yellow River thousands of years ago, leading to catastrophic floods that claimed millions of lives over time. Today the Three Rivers Project in China is the world's largest dam, with attendant horrific environmental consequences.

2. Quoted from Malcolm Quantrill, *Alvar Aalto: A Critical Study* (New York: Shocken, 1983), p. 5.

BIBLIOGRAPHY

The Architecture of Frank Lloyd Wright, by Neil Levine. Princeton, NJ: Princeton University Press, 1997.

The Art of War, by Sun Tzu, translated by Thomas Cleary. Boulder, CO: Shambala Dragon, 1988.

Between Heaven and Earth: A Guide to Chinese Medicine, by Harriet Beinfeld and Efrem Korngold. New York: Ballantine, 1991.

The Book of Nei Kung (Ch'i Kung), by C. K. Chu. New York: Sunflower, 1986.

Chinese Astrology: Interpreting the Revelations of the Celestial Messengers, by Derek Walters. London: Aquarian/Thorsons, 1993.

Chuang Tsu: Inner Chapters, translated by Gia-Fu Feng and Jane English. New York: Vantage, 1972.

The I Ching or Book of Changes, translated by Richard Wilhelm, rendered into English by Cary Baynes. Princeton, NJ: Princeton University Press, 1967.

Survey of Traditional Chinese Medicine, by Claude Larre, Jean Schatz, and Elisabeth Rochat de la Vallée. Columbia, MD: Traditional Acupuncture Institute, 1986.

T'ai Chi Ch'uan and Meditation, by Da Liu. New York: Shocken, 1986.

Tao: The Watercourse Way, by Alan Watts and Al Chung-Liang Huang. New York: Pantheon, 1977.

The Tao of Architecture, by Amos Ih Tiao Chang. Princeton, NJ: Princeton University Press, 1981.

Bibliography

The Tao of Health and Longevity, by Da Liu. New York: Marlowe, 1990.

Taoism: The Way of the Mystic, by J. C. Cooper. Wellingborough, England: Aquarian Press, 1990.

Tao Te Ching: The Definitive Edition, by Lao Tzu, with translation and commentary by Jonathan Star. New York: Jeremy P. Tarcher/Penguin, 2003.

Wabi-Sabi for Artists, Designers, Poets & Philosophers, by Leonard Koren. Berkeley, CA: Stone Bridge Press, 1994.

Wen-Tzu: Understanding the Mysteries, by Wen-Tzu, translated by Thomas Cleary. Boston: Shambhala Dragon Editions, 1991.

INDEX

Index

H

I

Index

ABOUT THE AUTHOR

Kurt Teske, a feng shui practitioner for more than twenty years, studied initially with the Taoist master Ta Liu in the 1980s and later with the first Geomancy Feng Shui Education Organization group at the New York Open Center. Teske has also studied traditional Chinese medicine, philosophy, and ch'i kung as well as architecture, history, film, and music. An Ohio native, he holds undergraduate and graduate degrees from Harvard and Columbia, where he studied philosophy, physics, and applied mathematics. He has been a member of the C. G. Jung Foundation for Analytical Psychology for more than two decades. He has collaborated with several Native American, environmental, and esoteric organizations, and has published works and filmed documentaries on a variety of topics, including a series of films on art and spirituality for the City University of New York.

About the Artist

A New Jersey native, Bil Leaf studied illustration and design at the Fashion Institute of Technology at the State University of New York in New York City, where he received both his Associates' and MFA degrees. He is a freelance designer and artist.